Visions of
Post-compul
Education

SRHE and Open University Press Imprint
General Editor: Heather Eggins

Visions of Post-compulsory Education

Edited by
Ian McNay

The Society for Research into Higher Education
& Open University Press

Published by SRHE and
Open University Press
Celtic Court
22 Ballmoor
Buckingham
MK18 1XW

and
1900 Frost Road, Suite 101
Bristol, PA 19007, USA

First published 1992

A catalogue record of this book is available from
the British Library

Library of Congress Cataloging-in-Publication Data

Visions of post-compulsory education / edited by Ian McNay.
 p.   cm.
 Includes bibliographical references (p.) and index.
 ISBN 0–335–09779–0–ISBN 0–335–09778–2 (pbk.)
 1. Post-compulsory education–Great Britain. I. McNay, Ian.
LC1039.8.G7V58 1992
378.41–dc20   91–45503
                                               CIP

Typeset in 10/11½ pt Baskerville
by Graphicraft Typesetters Ltd., Hong Kong
Printed in Great Britain by St Edmundsbury Press
Bury St Edmunds, Suffolk

Contents

Contributors

Judith Bell is a former HMI and college Vice-Principal.

Jennifer Bone is Assistant Director, Bristol Polytechnic.

David Bradshaw was Principal of Doncaster Metropolitan College and is working on the RSA project, 'Learning Pays', on 16–19 provision.

Robert Cuthbert is Assistant Director of Bristol Polytechnic.

John Gray is Principal of Basford Hall College, Nottingham.

David Hawkridge is Professor in the Institute of Education Technology at the Open University.

Ian McNay is Professor and Head of the Centre for Higher Education Management at Anglia Polytechnic.

David Morrell was formerly Registrar and Secretary, University of Strathclyde.

Leni Oglesby is President, European Bureau of Adult Education.

John Othick is Senior Lecturer in the Department of Economic and Social History, Queen's University, Belfast.

Alan Parker is Assistant Secretary (Education) at the Association of Metropolitan Authorities.

David Parkes and Gisela Shaw are at the European Institute of Education and Social Policy, Paris.

Tom Schuller is Director of the Centre for Continuing Education, University of Edinburgh.

Lorna Unwin is an independent trainer and consultant.

Preface and Acknowledgements

There is never a good time to prepare a book like this which has education policy as its focus. One of the pleas made in the text is for a better balance between continuity and change: the security given by the first is necessary to ensure the quality and validity of the second. The UK has not had that balance right in the recent past. Nor is it alone: political upheavals in Eastern Europe have been followed by projects for educational reform; Australia has restructured tertiary phase provision and the confrontation of the demands for growth, quality, relevance and accountability is universal.

A number of contributions in this collection have gone through several manifestations during its period of gestation – longer than usual because of acts of God and government. But, like the decision to invest in computers, where the 'between technologies syndrome' reflects delay in actual purchase because the next 'improvement' is always due out soon, somewhere a line has to be drawn and the 'go' decision made. It happened to come at the best of times and the worst of times: *three* White Papers and more legislation so soon after the 1988 Great Education Reform Act was supposed to have provided a settled basis for provision and control. I hope, I believe, the contributions here are a positive input to the debate about the form and content of post-school education in many of its varied forms which will continue as the end of the century approaches. In some details their starting points may have been passed but the principles are constant. Several, I believe, will grow in relevance: David Morrell's pleas for a return to a democratic, collective *professional* community, which is in harmony with changes now emerging in major companies who are abandoning macho hierarchies of executive control just as post-Jarratt universities are adopting them; Lorna Unwin's proposal for a professional body spanning educators *and* trainers (and can one government ministry spanning the two be far away in England?) and John Othick's internationalism which counters the Eurocentrism which could prevail in the years following 1992.

The contributions are in two major sections but they are not as discrete as that suggests. After a review of the 1980s, they are grouped as sector based and issue based but all draw on the past and present to examine possible futures; all are written by people with practical interests and involvement who have reached their views through reflection on their own, and others', experience; they attempt to relate UK experience to that of other countries and, in many cases, also make inter-sector comparisons. One of our weaknesses in the UK is to fail to disseminate lessons from varieties of experience, particularly when these cross sectors, but, for example, higher education needs to learn from adult education about mature students, Further Education colleges facing corporate status could learn not only from the Polytechnics and Colleges Funding Council sector but also schools which have 'opted out' to grant-maintained status. We hope that, at the end, readers see provision more holistically and can transfer others' experiential learning to their own context.

My thanks are due to fellow contributors and colleagues for their support, to a sterling band of secretaries who coped with scripts from those of us still between technologies, and to staff of Open University Press for their patience and skill as midwives.

Abbreviations

AE	Adult education
AMA	Association of Metropolitan Authorities
APL	Accreditation of prior learning
CAT	College of Advanced Technology
CATS	Credit accumulation and transfer systems
CBI	Confederation of British Industry
CDP	Committee of Directors of Polytechnics
CIHE	Council for Industry and Higher Education
CNAA	Council for National Academic Awards
COMETT	Community Action Programme for Education and Training for Technology
CTI	Computers in Teaching Initiative
CVCP	Committee of Vice-Chancellors and Principals
DENI	Department of Education, Northern Ireland
DES	Department of Education and Science
DTI	Department of Trade and Industry
EC	European Communities
EFTA	European Free Trade Area
EIESP	European Institute of Education and Social Policy
ERA	Education Reform Act
ERASMUS	European Community Action Scheme for the Mobility of University Students
FE	Further education
FEU	Further Education Unit
FS	Flexible specialization
GCB	General Colleges Budget
HE	Higher education
IT	Information technology
IPPR	Institute for Public Policy Research
LEC	Local Enterprise Company

LMC	Local Management of Colleges
MSC	Manpower Services Commission
NAB	National Advisory Body
NCVQ	National Council for Vocational Qualifications
NEDO	National Economic Development Organization
NIESR	National Institute for Economic and Social Research
NOW	New Opportunities for Women
NTI	New Training Initiative
PCFC	Polytechnics and Colleges Funding Council
PICKUP	Professional, Industrial and Commercial Updating
QTS	Qualified Teacher Status
RSA	Royal Society of Arts
SCOTVEC	Scottish Vocational Education Council
SEM	Single European market
TA	Training Agency
TC	Training Commission
TEC	Training and Enterprise Council
TEMPUS	Trans-European Mobility Scheme for University Studies
TES	*Times Educational Supplement*
TVEI	Technical and Vocational Education Initiative
UDACE	Unit for the Development of Adult Continuing Education
UFC	Universities Funding Council
UGC	University Grants Commission
VET	Vocational Education and Training
WEA	Workers' Educational Association
WRFE	Work-related Further Education
YTS	Youth Training Scheme

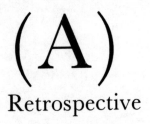

Retrospective

1

The 1980s: Change, Contradiction, Confusion and their Legacy

Ian McNay

Revolution or evolution?

In most revolutions there are periods where many of those affected must have wished for a U-turn, a reversion to the *status quo ante*: the Terror in France, Stalin's purges, the oppression and cultural desert of the Red Guard and Gang of Four period in China. The British Industrial Revolution brought, in the short term, increased poverty, slums and squalor. The current revolution in new technology is not the one sided good its enthusiastic evangelists suggest. It has a down side. For some it has meant deskilling or redundancy and many older people feel fearful of it, excluded by it and may blame it for the, perhaps coincidental, shift to a high base plateau of unemployment. Utopian rhetoric leads to dystopian reality. Revolutions are by their nature disruptive, dismissive of the good along with the bad, and discontinuities to development. More positively, such contrasts provoke an awareness of alternative scenarios and the possibility of a better informed choice of an evolutionary path. Evolution takes more notice of the necessary pace of productive and more harmonious change. This is, I hope, what the last decade of experimentation has done for the organism which is the system of post-compulsory education, training and development in the UK. It is now better prepared to adapt itself *from within* to the challenges of an approaching new century, in part by reflecting on its reaction, indeed resistance, to external attempts to impose change.

Much of this book starts with the present and looks forward. In this introductory chapter I look back briefly to examine some frameworks for analysis of policy and policy change and use these in an attempt to draw out key elements of the Thatcher revolutionary experiment.

The scope of policy

Sir Toby Weaver, the progenitor of the polytechnics and of their internal democracy prior to incorporation, has a salutory message for those who seek a Grand Plan, a Great Reform, which he encapsulates in a Law:

> The maximum speed with which it is possible to devise, negotiate and validate a central plan adequate to give each of some hundreds of institutions a practical guide to its tasks and a budget to support them, will always fall so far short of the speed of change in the situation with which it is designed to deal as to make the completed plan abortive.
>
> (Weaver, 1983)

Those of us advising on the early planning of the Open College warned that plans could be quick, or cheap or good. Two out of three would be unreasonable to expect; three, like Shredded Wheat, impossible. Government in the 1980s seemed not to have absorbed these lessons. It regularly attempted comprehensive change on short time-scales and came up with schemes that were poor and expensive. The Open College is slowly recovering from its premature launch, and other schemes were constantly reformulated to prevent rigorous comparisons, though even so not all the faults were corrected. There were some embarrassing evaluations of schemes which suffered from faults similar to the arrangements they displaced and which had been much derided. The National Audit Office (1987), commenting on the Adult Training Strategy, found that MSC had abandoned a costly intelligence system, had devised no reliable measure of employer training, produced statistics that contradicted its own claims on alleged skill shortages and sponsored a Skills Training Agency whose courses were more expensive than those in Further Education (FE) colleges. The Youth Training Scheme carried significant deadweight in being used by employers to gain state subsidy for what they had previously funded themselves (Deloitte, Haskins, Sells, 1987), and Department of Education and Science (DES) statistics showed that growth in traineeships under the scheme, at launch and when extended to two years, was almost exclusively at the expense of jobs with levels of unemployment among young people staying virtually unchanged (DES, 1990).

In higher education, again, realities did not seem to affect ideologies. The attraction of the USA model appeared to remain even after an HMI report (DES, 1989a) which showed that:

1. Costs per graduate were roughly three times higher in the USA in comparisons between two similar institutions.
2. Wastage rates on USA degree courses of over 50 per cent are common. On two year courses only *10* per cent of full-time students (and for part-timers only *2* per cent) completed successfully, even with a year's extension.
3. The annual bad debt write-off on student loans was US $1,500,000,000.

When wholesale reform was recognized as unmanageable, two strategies were adopted. The first was to divide the system by sector with schemes within each. This promoted inter-sector dissension, which may have been part of the hidden agenda with envy seen as a spur to competition. So universities were pressured to bring unit costs closer to those of polytechnics and colleges – and resisted. Their 'restructuring' costs were then covered more generously via such schemes as 'new blood' lectureships (an unfortunate label reinforcing 'cuts' and other surgical analogues). FE was a constant laboratory while A levels remained untouched and sixth forms protected when 'of proven worth' even though this created diseconomies for the rest of the system serving the majority population.

There were also discontinuities by *level*, especially in England and Wales. In Scotland, the Munn and Dunning reforms of 14–16 provision, and the development of the Action Plan to modularize vocational and professional education provision in further *and* higher education, have some coherent total rationality. South of the border, GCSE and the Technical Vocational Education Initiative (TVEI) created curricular discontinuities for those progressing to unreformed provision; as did the National Vocational Qualification (NVQ) initiative and the competence movement in articulation with higher education. This was not confined to 'top-down' initiatives: many students from local access courses were unprepared for an experience of higher education often at best indifferent to them and at times hostile to their expectations and their assertiveness over their needs.

The second strategy was to focus on policy areas. Weaver (1983) used a four-part categorization of policy areas which has stood well:

- *Access* – Who gets the opportunity?
- *Curriculum* – To study what?
- *Structure* – In what organizational framework?
- *Resources* – Funded by whom and how?

Again, there was an apparent failure to recognize the interdependence of these four – a point Weaver stresses – and surprise at the ripples of consequence in other areas or the demands provoked for congruent development, e.g. to resource access adequately.

Examples continue to proliferate; a few will suffice to illustrate the interdependence:

1. Increases in overseas fees to economic levels had an obvious access effect. As UK students found university entry harder, others pushed a more open door. Standards were compromised and new curricular ghettos developed, with course structures specifically and exclusively for overseas students. In universities such provision was the fastest growing area, in percentage terms, of any throughout the 1980s.
2. The nationalization without compensation (to the LEAs) of the polytechnics and other colleges created corporate enterprises whose financial strategy has meant a shift in their product portfolio (the new label for curriculum) to favour cost recovery courses mainly in professional development areas. There is a consequent shift in those gaining access, with some returning for more in an élite mode, possibly at the expense of more gaining first-time access to some – a mass mode (Trow, 1981). As with the

health service, commercial considerations take precedence over curriculum (clinical) need or community service. The same is likely to be true in FE, if funding of non-vocational adult education, often an access avenue because it is non-threatening, is discontinued.

3. The location of adult education within community and leisure directorates of local authorities also means that curriculum and clients change to match the norms of the structure, and fees become subject to VAT with obvious impact on access.

Models for change

Weaver's final contribution to this chapter is his identification (Weaver, 1979) of how government attempts to shift policy. Apart from the 'power of the purse', he lists:

1. *Information* – Research findings, reports of commissions, statistical trends indicate where adjustments are necessary.
2. *Exhortation* – Appeals by ministers, HMI, civil servants via meetings and the media urge adoption of a particular approach.
3. *Legislation* – Weaver saw this as a last resort in its full sense but circulars, orders in council, new regulations, act as quasi-legislation. The Robbins Report, the designation of polytechnics, and the closure of colleges of education were all pursued with hardly a debate in parliament, never mind legislation. In the 1980s there was more educational legislation than in any similar period. This reflects the regrettable collapse of consensual partnership. The 1988 Education Reform Act was thought to be the culmination of this litigious phase and contrasted with France 20 years earlier: there the people provoked and proposed legislation and government acted; here government proposed legislation and provoked the people to act so that, gradually, much of the framework of that Act is being dismantled. For post-16 provision, the Further and Higher Education Acts suggest that legislation may be becoming the normal mode of change management by government.

Weaver's categories echo Chin and Benne's three approaches to change (1976):

1. *empirical – rational*
2. *normative – re-educative*
3. *power – coercive*

which Miller *et al.* (1986) gloss in the context of a (somewhat idealized) college:

1. Things get done because powerful influences are able to impose decisions – for example, if you want a decision made in your favour, persuade the Vice-Principal.

2. Things get done because, when presented with clear objective information and argument, people will decide in a rational way – for example, if you undertake research, present findings and carefully constructed conclusions, then everyone will agree to the presented solution.
3. Things get done through a process of reflection and review of existing practice, leading to mutually agreed changes in behaviour, attitudes and objectives – for example, if you give all the staff the opportunity to take part in discussing the need for change, then agreement will be reached.

Would that consensus and common commitment were so easy in the real world! At institutional level resolutions of Council, Senate or Academic Board equate to legislation, with memos from senior staff as quasi-circulars. In simple terms forces for change act on the body, the brain, or the heart–soul. And, of course, the exhortation which at national level is labelled propaganda to win hearts and minds, in colleges becomes 'staff development'!

Becher and Kogan (1992) add structure to process. They postulate a hierarchical model with four levels:

1. central
2. institutional
3. unit
4. individual.

I believe 'central' is still a deficient label to cover what they spread it over and prefer 'external'. The model adapts easily to application internally to institutions by losing central/external and adding an 'activity' level given the emergent importance of course and project teams (McNay, 1989a). In their model, change is necessary to preserve or restore a 'dynamic equilibrium' both between levels and between the 'normative' and 'operational' modes at each level. If the behaviour of an entity – the way it acts – is out of line with its values, the way it thinks, then one or other has to change. This may be true at lower levels, but hasn't seemed to work at governmental level where examples proliferate of paradox between the rhetoric of policy and the reality of practice:

1. Proclaiming college freedom to use entrepreneurial income but reducing baseline grants to force them to generate such income to cover existing commitment.
2. Advocating a 'free market' approach with customer choice . . . until students make 'wrong' choices despite interference with the market by grant inducements in preferred areas.
3. Claiming to 'roll back the frontiers of the state' but preventing decisions of local democracies being implemented (e.g. on tertiary reorganization) and extending government involvement into curriculum content and processes (e.g. training of teachers of reading, marking standards for A level spelling).
4. Castigating universities' abuse of autonomy, commending LEA sponsorship of development in higher education, but legislating for LEA colleges

to move to a structure and system of control parallel with that of universities which it had threatened to amend.

Within the model, the lever for change is to introduce an imbalance at some
point and let it work its way through. Becher and Kogan suggest that
connections cannot leap levels but central funding through individuals will
no doubt change institutional policy. Most major change has been top down:
in finance the requirement for efficiency indicators; the emergence of new
structures via the Manpower Services Commission (MSC), Training Agency
(TA) or TECs as alternatives to the LEAs and new curriculum initiatives such
as TVEI, the Youth Training Scheme (YTS) and the Enterprise in Higher
Education scheme as well as specific funding of new blood in e.g. biotechnology. Access has been the main 'bottom up' area of change. Curricular
innovations through new course proposals, and cooperative structures via consortia and, ultimately, mergers have started in the middle levels of the model.

The government's psychology has been a mix of Skinner and Pavlov. Its
meretricious approach assumes everybody has their price and they have
provided specific funds for specific behaviour in the operational mode. If
academics push the right levers to stimulate government's ideological plea-
sure zones there is delivery of the necessities for survival. Even academics
have basic instincts and learn to push the right levers. Their vanity and
intelligence then require them to resolve the ensuing cognitive dissonance by
embracing government rhetoric and espoused values in a way which has
more basis in rationalization than ratiocination.

Perhaps the most satisfactory model to illuminate policy change over the
past decade or more is that of contingency theory (Bruton, 1987), which
allows a pragmatic plotting of ends, and the degree of agreement on them,
against means and how far they are proven to guarantee delivery. If ends are
agreed and means to their delivery proven, planning is rational. If means to
particular ends are proven but there is no agreement on those ends, political
negotiation ensues, usually leading to a range of initiatives to accommodate
diverse missions in our pluralist world. If ends are not agreed nor means
proven there is chaos, with a need to define problems and clarify processes.
These last two carry elements of the organized anarchy and 'garbage-can'
processes of Cohen and March (1983) where solutions stand ready to be
fitted to problems in a fluid and unpredictable decision-making process.

It is the fourth quadrant that appeals: if ends are agreed but means are
unproven, the cause–effect relationship is not established or secure. There is,
therefore, a learning process to undergo: planning is preceded by experimentation, a series of trials and errors. The system and the service are
treated like a laboratory fruit-fly (*Drosophila melanogaster*) – legs added
here, wing span extended, body weight adjusted and, in time, some of those
may persist in successive generations. To me that encapsulates the 1980s, a
period when novelty took precedence over quality, and there was an impati-
ence for results at fruit-fly speed as ministers sought to bolster their cabinet
c.v. by having an eponymous scheme. The mad scientist syndrome gains

further credibility as a vision when Lord Young's memoirs confirm that several such schemes were whimsical musings aloud when seized upon for launch after some minimal development work.

Contradiction and confusion

Such factors led to a pervasive short-termism which not only militates against developmental investment to improve quality – and excellence needs the security of continuity to thrive – but carries an inevitable inefficiency. Short-term funding reduces commitment and does not stimulate performance to gain extension (Martin, 1985), and the lack of a clear framework and reasonable planning horizon made the environment in which institutions work even harder to analyse. The Jarratt Report (CVCP, 1985) recorded that the major contributing factor to institutions' problems in managing efficiently was the uncertainty created by the government's own lack of planning and its inconsistent policy stance.

There was, as already noted, contradiction between the rhetoric and reality of policy. There was also conflict between policies. Part of this lay in the struggle for control of education when its primary role was seen as a service agent to the economy so that education policy was subordinate to economic and, particularly, employment policy. Employers were expected to fund part-time students, especially for mid-career development, but the structures to encourage this by a levy in line with many of our EC partners were dismantled. The 16–19 jungle was not cleared by competing schemes proliferating from the DES and the Department of Employment (DE) with some Department of Trade and Industry (DTI) involvement. Replan, Restart and others were on offer from different perspectives to the unemployed.

Even within the DES there were contradictions. LEA planning of 16–19 provision – where tertiary structures are more efficient and effective – was hampered first by Sir Keith Joseph's protection of academic enclaves in school sixth forms, then by the opt-out provision used by any school reacting petulantly out of narrow self-interest to changes for the greater good, then by the 1991 White Papers provoked by the need to reduce poll tax bills (HMSO, 1991a,b). So the tyranny of minorities undermined the planning urged on others but specifically eschewed for government by Kenneth Baker in a speech at Lancaster in January 1989 with the sub-theme of 'can't plan, won't plan'. Yet others' plans are not accepted either.

There were, too, some dramatic U-turns. In that same speech, Baker had a vision of higher education provision at the end of the century with twice the student numbers then participating. Previously a Green Paper (HMSO, 1985) had envisaged the possible closure of some institutions in a rationalization of decremental contraction. When universities took arts students on a fees-only basis after the 1981 UGC cuts, fees were instantly halved so they came below marginal costs. Now universities are urged to take such fees-only students and fees have more than doubled to make such a strategy attractive.

Continuities?

I've suggested that experiments were based on agreed ends. I can distinguish four over-arching aims. These are not exclusive to education, they have applied to transport, housing, health and other areas. They echo Weaver's four policy areas:

1. *Value for money* – Neave (1988) suggests that many states have now moved to monitoring output from higher education and reduced the emphasis on input as investment in favour of cost per product. As the Green Paper put it in accepting the reformulation of the 'Robbins principle' on access to higher education as potential to benefit: 'so long as taxpayers substantially finance higher education, the benefit has to be sufficent to justify the cost' (HMSO, 1985).
2. *Throughput* – The adoption of access as a buzzword by government came late. More, even of the same, was the important issue – *big* numbers. There was only a secondary commitment to more meaning different, and no recognition that quality suffered. The big growth in the 1980s came at postgraduate and professional levels, where, significantly, a higher proportion of students is privately financed. As with the health service a two tier system is emerging.
3. *Privatization/secularization* – Vocationalism was *in*. Not a new issue – there is a ten-year cycle of attempts at exhortation and legislation: the Barlow Report (1946), *Technical Education* (1956), the Polytechnics White Paper (1966), Callaghan's 1976 Ruskin speech and its aftermath, the DeVille report on National Vocational Qualifications (1986), but this time there was sustained pressure. The temples of learning and their priests were derided and their control passed to the 'laity'; a non-conformist alternative was sponsored with accredited work-based learning and experiential learning. A new curriculum linked to competence and enterprise was devised. There are parallels in the real church where home worship thrives, and in theatre where the vitality is in community and street activity, not in the traditional centres.
4. *Structural elimination of the 'alternative state'* – Local authorities were *out*: from housing, from urban renewal, from transport, from education. In FE their plans had to be endorsed by MSC/TA/TECs who were given a 'golden share' control of 25 per cent of budgets. In adult education much provision closed as budgets were squeezed and capped. Higher education was nationalized and further education has had cut its umbilical cord to the representatives of the communities which nurtured it (HMSO, 1991a,b).

Adversity and diversity

This impressionistic sketch brings us to the question – what now? My view from working with a number of institutions across all sectors is that there is a new assertiveness abroad. It may be a reaction to being messed around so much, or a new maturity which working through adversity brings. Institutions now seem ready to decide for themselves, to determine their mission(s), to declare their distinctiveness, and take responsibility for themselves. They are taking the government's urging to be entrepreneurial at face value, which may be a bluff-calling strategy. Paradoxically, centralization may help this; hitherto there have been checks on venture management, usually sufficient. With over 500 potential corporations under central control this will be less easy: if one is pushed down, two others will bob up elsewhere. With any risk investments, of course, some will go down, others up, but institutions have, too, become aware of their strength. There is a growing recognition that education is a key to a prosperous future; that government needs them as much as vice versa. They are not parasites on the economy but symbiotes in its development, unwilling to take the blame for government underinvestment relative to our EC partners; and increasingly they look to Europe for funds. They have found, too, a collective strength illustrated by the concerted resistance to the Universities Funding Council (UFC) bidding process. There was a point where the sectors seemed fissiparous as the competitive ethic was urged and polytechnic directors in their corporations behaved like leaders of newly independent republics.

That, mercifully, seems to have passed and diversity and collectivity seem to have melded to produce a renewed commitment to their various communities. The views that follow in succeeding chapters convey some of this though others, particularly from the universities, suggest the watershed is not yet passed, the crisis not yet purged.

(B)
Perspective: Views from Interested Parties

2

Universities: Responsibility and Motivation

David Morrell

Introduction

There is a Scottish tradition that education is so important that all members of the family must be prepared to make sacrifices to ensure that the most able of the children can benefit from it to the limits of their capacity. In the 1960s and 1970s the UK seemed to be following that policy as a national family. There was popular support for the government in investing in higher education. Thousands of the more able and enterprising members of families with no previous experience or expectation of higher education sacrificed well-paid employment opportunities to live on student grants and seek the longer term benefits of higher education. They constitute the substantial body of graduate scientists, engineers, managers, mothers and others whose efforts (along with North Sea Oil) allow the present level of national prosperity and civilization.

During the process of expansion there was inevitable social turbulence and disorientation. There were policy mistakes, extravagances, and some self-indulgence. The negative aspects attracted media attention and penetrated the public consciousness. The 1980s, then, saw the reaction against the concept of the less able making sacrifices for the benefit of the more able as a long-term investment for the general good. Instead emphasis was laid upon notions of self-help and competition that were thought to have been the basis of national prosperity in earlier times.

Needs and expectations

In attempting to look ahead the principal questions must be to ascertain what the nation will expect, who will be responsible for focusing these expectations into policies, and how the policy objectives can be successfully achieved. Pressures for fundamental change in what constitutes the British nation will greatly intensify. This will happen in two directions: the drive towards European union and increasing demand for regional devolution – see Chapters 8 and 14. A second assumption about the 1990s is that while there are great pressures and expectations in the direction of greater private funding recognizing that the dependence of institutions upon public funding has been greatly reduced, a significant element of the cost of higher education will continue to be financed by taxpayers. (Even proposals involving fee paying via student vouchers depend upon public funding of the vouchers.)

So, the British taxpayers' expectations are the expectations that we must analyse. In the most general terms these expectations might be summed up as the promotion of the further evolution of civilized society and the provision of adequate material means to support that society.

We must confront, therefore, considerations of the general concept of quality of life and the wealth creation needed to support it. In earlier times a nation was considered to be prosperous when it had some rich people, a considerable number of people in comfortable circumstances, and many poor people. We now expect that a prosperous nation will have some rich, most comfortable, and inevitably some poor. If that is to be achieved on a continuous basis the aspirations of individuals, which constitute the essential source of dynamism, must be maintained or increased. Poor may aspire strongly to improve their lot. Comfortable may aspire to remain comfortable. Does this provide the same level of dynamism? Currently efforts are being made to free up the force inherent in enlightened self-interest and thereby to encourage the aspiration to be rich. However, one cannot assume that everyone equates quality of life with wealth. It is very possible that the majority, already comfortable, will prefer to promote their quality of life in other ways. As the proportion of the population enjoying higher education increases this seems even more likely to be the case.

But, it will be argued, without the drive to be economically rich, the country will fail to compete and will become poor. So, it seems necessary to question further the concept of wealth and prosperity. At the personal level is a person who has contrived to concentrate material resource under their control thereby a wealth creator? Is it possible that a devoted teacher who has inspired several hundred successful careers or an altruistic discoverer or inventor, who has forgotten to patent work, should not be considered to be a wealth creator? Wealth creators and wealth seekers are not always the same people.

The aspirations of individuals today are becoming more qualitative than economic but in the achievement of imaginative and creative concepts individuals will find the new drive for aspiration and will also be productive of ideas, goods and services.

Small nations with strong traditions of support for education over a substantial period of time are almost axiomatically nations of high quality of life. Scotland and Wales show such signs but are submerged within a larger nation where the majority tradition has laid less emphasis upon education and which, until the middle of this century, showed an élitist attitude towards it. To this day Scotland has more young people per head of population who aspire to higher education, who succeed in it, and who go on to be more valuable and productive citizens as a result.

Individual aspirations are unaffected by current political cultures. There are clear reasons for being concerned about the relationship between the dip in the number of young people and the need for a highly educated and trained workforce. The aspirations of the 1960s and 1970s are shadowed in the children of the 1960s graduates – but it is a shadow without the same force. The political policies of the 1980s were less than inadequate in the face of this problem. In the 1990s entirely new attitudes and new policies will be essential if the national expectations are to be fulfilled.

College or company?

The universities of the UK received two salutary shocks in the 1980s which gave effect to the national disappointment at the failure of investment in higher education to achieve expectations. In 1981 an overall 15 per cent reduction in funding removed much of the scope for extravagance and self-indulgence. In 1985–88 there was a much more profound, and difficult to interpret, culture shock. Words and concepts had their meanings changed. Enterprise and management were good: welfare and consensus were bad. This was not a process of questioning, of argument or of persuasion. It was a process of assertion, revealed solutions and presentations.

The Jarratt Report (CVCP, 1985) began from the assumption that committees were inherently unsound: expensive, indecisive, dilatory and irresponsible. However, the analysis was superficial and the verdict was an over-reaction. *Some* academic committees *were* costly, ineffective and difficult to wind up, but some committee systems were well structured, effective, speedy and well led. Such systems represented communication and participation in a peculiarly effective form. The absolute destruction of committees (often replaced almost immediately by 'management groups') meant that with the bathwater of committees have gone out the babies of consensus, involvement and identification with policy. These gave a vital element of meaning and purpose not just to the committee members but also to their colleagues in the outlying departments of what are inherently centrifugal institutions. It is not altogether surprising that the commercial members of the Jarratt Committee did not foresee this result. However, comparative studies of the level of identification and involvement of employees with corporate objectives in Japanese industry might have sounded a warning note.

Universities have thrived through the ages as collegiate organizations: groups of scholars attracting students or groups of students employing scholars. The traditional basis *may* not be the best for modern times but the question was never asked. The 'individual in the community' aspect of academic life has been fundamental. There are vital reasons why it must continue to be so if universities are to continue to be effective. In place of this collegiate ethos, of which we have so much experience, a system of management, which already seems out of date in its original context, is now being imported. Such a system inevitably concentrates and centralizes power and authority through individuals in a hierarchy. This centralization demands a mechanism to counter it which takes the form of structured devolution. Power is therefore theoretically re-delegated on a conditional and accountable basis. However, that is not how it appears on the receiving end, particularly in the context of shrinking budgets. There, the perception is that central authority divides the resources and sets the targets and is thereafter in a position to delegate the responsibility for the achievement of the targets without necessarily providing the means for their achievement. At the grass roots it is known who will be blamed for non-achievement; however, there is little hope of the benefits of grass roots knowledge and experience penetrating objectively through the individual hierarchy to inform central authority. Failures are apt to be blamed by the top upon underperformance and by the bottom upon underfunding. The scene is set for acrimonious deadlock.

Management operates through concepts of rewards (performance-related pay, for example) and penalty (hence the need to remove security of tenure). Good management may, by presentation and exhortation, attempt to get across ideas of organizational goals and missions but employees need not be involved in their formulation or modification.

In attempting to apply this model to a higher education institution a number of problems immediately arise. Academic managers at all levels are not in fact subject to summary dismissal. Effective incentives to active academics are different from, and often much more expensive than those offered to company executives. Academic staff are normally highly self-motivated specialists and extremely individualistic. They have to be led not managed, they have to be persuaded and not ordered (Handy, 1983). Their individual competitors are more likely to be in other institutions rather than among their own colleagues. They may ignore management views of their performance and can often afford to do so as their performance is itself individualistic and not wholly to be judged in the context of their employment. They can easily become divorced from institutional purpose and goals, and are liable to do so if antagonized (see Chapter 3). When this happens the consequences for students and for such matters as much needed reforms of course structure and content can be adverse. Resistance to change becomes hardened and the manager wonders why.

It is particularly important that grass roots experience and sentiment be heard quietly, continuously and clearly at the highest levels. That was one of the functions of an effective committee system in which clear and direct speaking was encouraged. The balance between participative consensus and authoritarian management will, in my view, profoundly affect the effectiveness of individual institutions of higher education in the next ten years.

Autonomy, accountability, efficiency and effectiveness

When the University Grants Commission (UGC) (advisory) was replaced by the UFC (statutory) appearances seemed to indicate a strengthening of the buffer function and therefore a stronger defence of institutional autonomy.

Lord Chilver addressing the Conference of University Administrators in 1989 stated that the UFC would consult universities, formulate its own aims simply 'to form a back-drop and a set of criteria against which the Council will develop its policy and make funding decisions', and 'encourage universities to exercise their autonomy'.

However, the UFC would also ensure 'that the university sector develops ways which lead to high quality and cost-effective institutions which play their part in meeting national needs . . .'. A complex system of negotiation of specific funding for universities was to be operated with a 'minimum of bureaucracy'.

The interests of the government's views of national priorities and the interests of institutional autonomy are clearly in conflict. The balance is clear and inclines towards the current government view of national needs and expectations.

Griffiths (1989) sees the universities being required 'to subordinate their academic purposes to centrally determined ends'. The Secretary of State for Education and Science in the new structure may 'impose on the UFC any supplementary functions he thinks fit' and may insist that the UFC 'comply with any directions' given. Griffiths accuses the Vice Chancellors and Principals with losing their legitimate authority by behaving as individuals rather than delegates of their institutions, with accepting unquestioningly the 'chief executive' role thrust upon them by the Jarratt Report and thereby becoming surrogates of the Secretary of State in a national management structure for higher education. It would not be the first time in human history that increased authority was seen as the antidote to failure of leadership.

Griffiths perceives the rule of law (determined by consensus) being replaced by personal patronage (exercised by managers) and bureaucratic instruments (memoranda and audits) and he hints at the ominous possibilities of centralized control of academic decisions including those on course content. It remains to be seen whether any 'merged' structure of higher education will be subject to similar pressures, but it seems likely since the college sector is more accustomed to them than the universities.

One need not accept much of this analysis to be concerned at the nature, speed, and direction of change. Politicians and civil servants argued that all that is expected is that adequate accountability for the expenditure of considerable public funding, similar to that normal in other areas, be established. They protested that the powers now created are not expected to be necessary or to be used. (Is this not typical of the attitudes of incipient tyranny?) The fact is that an apparatus for central political control has been deliberately created where one did not exist before. How can it be guaranteed that no future government, whatever its politics, will abuse that power?

As Griffiths says, 'the boundary line between holding a body to financial account and indicating the ways in which it should spend its money is notoriously difficult to draw'.

University constitutions are littered with the debris of obsolete mechanisms of reassurance such as the post of Visitor, the General Councils or Convocations, Academic Assemblies and so on. Their existence demonstrates the need for reassurance against alien and potentially hostile powers which have been felt in the past. Where there is no shelter will there be any blossom or harvest?

The original block grant system was an incredible act of trust. That trust was sometimes abused but the results were admired throughout the world. Trust and accountability are parts of the same quantity. More accountability means less trust. Institutions that are not trusted will not be able to be as original, as creative, and as diverse. To achieve support they will be required to conform to systems, aims, and policies.

Higher education systems that are openly and directly administered under government do not have to be trusted; responsibility is seen to rest with government. Institutions in such a system can enjoy advantages (security of tenure as civil servants) as well as suffer disadvantages (policy control). A system that pretends to trust but does not actually do so is not only dishonest but is vulnerable to the twin evils of centralized control (which ensures that all errors are committed on a national scale) and loss of institutional consciousness and self-confidence. The danger must be that the nation will find itself with results that may be generally satisfactory but seldom excellent.

Options in systems

Some believe that the choices before institutions could include complete autonomy achieved through privatization. Theoretically the payment by students of economic fees (presumably financed by even larger loans) together with the receipt of research funding could finance an institution within which the academic community would enjoy a real autonomy. In such circumstances accountability would be diffused towards thousands of faceless customers who unless effectively organized, would be unlikely to express any coherent demands. Without the normal constitutional safeguards the scene could be set for a considerable degree of academic irresponsibility and even self-indulgence. However, the basic economic fact is that the scale of funding involved is so great that, through whatever route it is channelled, the public via government will have to contribute and will expect accountability.

The second possibility is a state university system giving ultimate control and complete reassurance to government and civil servants but with some guarantees for academic independence. This operates well in many countries.

The third possibility is that the universities should ultimately insist upon the preservation of their own institutional integrity in the belief that this is the best way to pursue their ultimate aims. If they do so they will have to decide whether the vitality, vigour, and success they have demonstrated in the past (both in teaching and research) was due more to generous funding or to collegiate partnership.

If they go along with the pressures of the 1980s believing they have to accept the inevitable, they are going to lose both funding and partnership. Because the quality of the past achievements is accepted, even by the most persistent of critics, to have been high in both absolute and comparative terms it is easy to fall into the trap of seeming to wish to set the clock back. That cannot be. Much has already been destroyed. New understandings and new cultures need time to grow and they will not begin to grow until trust is re-established and threats and harassments cease.

Dynamics and structures for change

We have seen how the nation will need a highly competent and highly civilized population to even maintain the quality of life into the next century. Fewer producers of goods and services will have to support more elderly and young people in the face of ever-increasing competition. Natural resources will be diminished. Wealth creation will depend upon high quality of products supported by high technology and high integrity. Education and training provision as presently under resourced and demoralized, is quite unprepared for this challenge. Other countries are investing but more importantly also seem to have a sense of shared mission from national to individual level which we lack. The motivation of every person in higher education is the critical factor behind any possibility of doing more with less. Staff feel denigrated, harassed, under-valued and exploited. These feelings must be turned round from the negative to the positive. Appeals to a sense of responsibility, to challenge, even to self-denial, would be hypocritical and non-credible in the climate that has been created.

Each profession has felt the denigration inherent in the current emphasis on competition and profit. Professions are private bodies with public privileges and responsibilities. Their position is a classical component of the concept of freedom with responsibility – freedom, in particular, from the ever-increasing power of the state. There is a feeling that there is not only a withdrawal of trust from the academic profession but a reneging from this ancient and important contract upon which some of our most treasured liberties are based. It can be argued that in a free society free individuals and autonomous associations of free individuals must be enabled, encouraged, and trusted to do what is required within the limits of the simplest and easiest audit possible. Academe is not a machine that can be driven by government, UFC, or managers, anywhere – other than into the ground.

What, therefore, can be done to adapt universities effectively? The time is ripe for a radical review of the classical form of charters and statutes. A new model charter would ensure a proper balance between authority and responsibility.

What might emerge would be a modern version of the collegiate concept, under effective lay government, academically led and professionally served. These are the components upon which the institutional consciousness and loyalty must be based if all members of the institution are each to make their best contributions towards the effectiveness of the institution as a whole.

The system of governance and administration must be able to cope with diversity without unnecessary constraints upon it. However, the component of strong personal motivation towards a mission with which each member of the community can identify is the essential dynamic that the context of governance and administration must nourish.

Under recent pressures there has been a failure to separate the process of policy determination from that of management. It is necessary to have effective lay and staff participation (in carefully assessed balance and in context) in determining policy. Management has a duty to inform the policy-making process and to execute the policy decisions. It has never been the management role in this context to *make* the policy decision. The attempt to import wholesale concepts of management from a very different context has brought about confusion and resentment. Efforts to design institutional mission statements have been frustrated in bland generalities because of the vast range of personal goals involved. Attempts to identify simple means of measuring institutional effectiveness have so far resulted in an over-emphasis on what is quantifiable.

Some missionaries of change have not realized that the culture they are attempting to import is much more rigid, formal, and resistant to further change, than the classical context that they would cast aside or ignore.

New ways will have to be found to pursue economy, efficiency and effectiveness in universities. What is meant is the economy which is the result of trusting, able, conscientious, and hard-working individuals to make the most of their talents with a minimum of structure and monitoring. The efficiency which is achieved from the willing and enthusiastic efforts of personnel who identify with collective aims because of involvement and participation in their definition. The effectiveness of members in a community who understand and accept that the success of the community and their own personal fulfilment are ultimately inseparable.

What is required is an array of flexible and interlinked courses provided by institutions working in partnership with government, employers, each other and others. They need to be widely responsive and to operate in a dominating climate of partnership within which there would still be scope for competition. The ideologies of egalitarianism and of market need to be set aside to allow progress governed by pragmatic common sense.

However, the true cost of educating at this level significantly more than 20 per cent of the age group is being seen by government as being more than the taxpayer is prepared to meet. Therefore contributions to this cost must be sought as widely as possible. Different mechanisms of cost contribution will be appropriate to different sources. Employers who need the qualified personnel must contribute, enterprises which exploit research, discovery and development must contribute, graduates whose lifetime earnings are above average must contribute. Those who are far sighted enough to wish to make disinterested donations must be given every incentive to do so. However, all of these contributors also pay taxes and each of them will continue to expect that the major contribution should come via the democratic processes from the product of these taxes.

To ensure that they are adequate the government will have the task, with every assistance institutions can render, of bringing forcibly to public attention the direct connection between investment in non-compulsory education and future national prosperity.

Universities and markets

A marketing approach is implied, and this means convincing clients to buy a product which will benefit them. This 'marketing' concept is another aspect of 'new management' being promoted at the institutional level.

Universities deal in many different markets. They are in the market as customers for staff and in that context used to offer some freedom, some challenge, some opportunity, and a standard of living comparable with that of other employees with similar qualifications. Now it would appear that they offer great challenge, much sweat, some tears, and a declining standard of living.

Universities are in the market as the purveyors of the outcome of research and development and have learned hard lessons in recent years from venture capitalists, exploiters of technology, and other skilled and ruthless participants in that game, shedding in the process much of their altruistic innocence.

Universities are in yet another market as purveyors of educated and trained people where they have made great strides in the design of new and flexible undergraduate curricula and of vocationally oriented graduate courses. (It was an accepted academic attitude as late as the mid-1960s in some universities that course design should be deliberately unrelated to vocational considerations.)

In the next few years universities will be in competition in the market for new students. Consciousness of the importance of the student market began well before there was any danger of shortage of applicants. Prospectuses and open days were developed over 20 years ago to help students make better informed choices. Demographic information was a starting point for the old quinquennial planning process. It was university administrators who first drew attention to the 'children of the 1960s graduates factor' in forecasting demand for places. However, this market is now becoming competitive. Money is being spent to influence rather than merely to inform student choice. Prestige, quality, and appropriateness of courses are factors of choice – in that order. Perceptions are being influenced by public relations budgets rather than objective advice.

Universities may be tempted to admit students who should be at college thus starving vitally important college courses of good entrants. The need to ease the flow of student transfer between institutions during courses will be much greater and this will have its own implications for flexibility of course design and for credit transfer.

Pure market thinking assumes selfish motivations. Students must be allowed to choose selfishly because the system exists for their benefit. But do institutions have a right to be selfish in the same way as profit making concerns? Even 'ethical' investments are marketed on the basis of capital and income return. Can educational institutions act analogously? The markets of education exist, must be recognized, and must be responded to. However, in the end, the motivation of the personnel in the system must have an element of non-market unselfishness. This element of calling, of commitment, of devotion, and of dedication is essential if the staff are to continue to function effectively at below market cost.

National needs and expectations – future

It is appropriate to return to the question of the nature of national expectations of higher education. In Britain 60 per cent of children abandon full-time education at the age of 16 compared with 10 per cent in Germany and the USA and 4 per cent in Japan. In the 1990s able young people leaving school will, because they will be a scarce commodity, receive very tempting offers to enter directly into paid employment. Add to this the fact that considerable damage has been done to successful selective secondary schools by political dogmas of various kinds in the last 30 years. The resulting skills shortages of the 1990s (foreseen by university planners in the early 1980s) have the makings of a national disaster. Britain's continuing adherence to élitist concepts of further and higher education and employer neglect of training is resulting in a totally under-equipped work force which could lead to as many as 200,000 responsible and influential appointments in European industry and commerce being occupied by non-British rather than British personnel after 1992.

Government has begun to recognize the danger and now has a policy of wider access. The end has been defined but what about the means? Increases in wages offered to school leavers are already evident and are not likely to be overcome by the student loan scheme presently on offer. Many families unfamiliar with higher education and with only brief experience of a higher standard of living behind them are now faced with substantial parental contributions. These contributions are not mandatory and the incidence of non-payment will increase further. Government remains determined to contribute less per student to the cost of higher education. Private support for the teaching element of higher education is negligible and unlikely to rise significantly.

Of the resources available for higher education in the UK a much higher proportion than in comparable countries is spent on student support. Because the total available is likely to remain severely constrained priority dictates that some of these funds must be diverted to the direct cost of higher education. There are other models of student loans systems more cost effective than the one being implemented. What might be more acceptable is the concept of an involuntary contribution to the higher education of future generations payable by graduates over a working lifetime from a very small percentage of their earnings.

However, that diversion of recurrent funding would only be a contribution towards the total required. What is necessary is the establishment of mechanisms to relate and monitor the returns on investment over the generations (because that is the time-scale of such investment). The matter is urgent but until government is prepared to describe higher education expenditure as investment rather than cost it seems unlikely that the general public will begin to understand the dangers of underinvestment. Employers must be encouraged to take a longer view and to subscribe to training at a realistic and comparable level. A whole category of invaluable institutes of technology is financed in France by employers spending vouchers raised through a general levy. Compulsion has the merit of spreading the load fairly over all and not just exploiting the willing and foresighted.

Higher education institutions must in return be prepared to offer guarantees and monitoring of the effectiveness of institutional performance. That these can be provided without harmful restrictions on academic and institutional freedoms is being gradually established. However, they will only work effectively if they are devised through consultation and not imposed.

The US context is often quoted as a free market economy which displays the potential of private initiative and private funding in higher education. However, when the relevant time-scale is applied it can be seen that American employers are presently reaping the rewards of more than a century of massive public investment. The USA already has much of the infra-structure that Britain so badly lacks. Moreover, it has a culture and tradition of mass participation in higher education that it will take much more than pious concern over access to induce in this country. American society was not built upon the desire of a few to get very rich but upon the aspirations and efforts of the many (mostly in waves of immigrants) to achieve a decent level of life in a climate that offered both democracy and opportunity.

Having looked briefly at a main aspect of the needs of the nineties (and there are many more including the whole question of the erosion of the research base) it is necessary to look at the choices and who must make them. The expansion of the 1960s and 1970s, with their errors and excesses, has set going a pendulum of public perception which has swung back with a vengeance. A balance needs to be sought between the imperatives of funding and the needs of the community that is expected to provide the funds. If one believes that the national government, in an imperfect democratic system such as ours, has a monopoly of wisdom, then a case for strong government steering of higher education can be made. However, given the remoteness of government from regions and institutions, the enormously sensitive local antennae of most institutions, and their international contacts at many levels, they have at least as much chance of getting policy right as any central authority.

Given the possibility for each member of an institution to contribute to the shaping of its policies and priorities the relationship to the community around it can be very sensitive indeed. Institutional autonomy with effective participation can contribute directly to both institutional responsiveness and effectiveness.

If the trends towards more personal and less public responsibility and towards more academic and less pragmatic management continue, the powerful public service motivation will have inadequate scope, and university administration will no longer attract some of the 'brightest and best'. The implications of this for the effectiveness of universities in the future should be examined through a more objective analysis than I can provide. However, it does seem ironical that the threat of academic anarchy inherent in the overpowerful senates (in certain universities) in the 1960s should be followed in the 1980s and 1990s by a threat of academic oligarchy. It reminds one forcibly that university constitutions were carefully designed to provide a maximum element of academic freedom within an ultimate constraint of public interest. The academic community is being its own worst enemy if it attempts to break out of this wise and generous context in the direction of either anarchy or oligarchy. The one lesson I would draw for the 1990s is that the councils and senates must stand firm on their constitutional rights and responsibilities and resist alien and inappropriate doctrines being pressed from either inside or outside. Unless they do so the balance between public and academic interest will again be seen to be swinging towards the latter and hope of a return of public confidence in the support of universities will be reduced once again.

3

The Exploding Community?
The University Idea and the
Smashing of the Academic Atom[1]

Tom Schuller

Introduction

> Oneness and wholeness are of the very essence of man's will to know. In
> practice this oneness and wholeness is realized only in specialized fields,
> yet these very specialties are not alive except as members of a single
> body of learning. Integration of the various disciplines joins them into a
> cosmos which culminates in the vision of a unified science, in theology,
> and in philosophy.   (Jaspers, 1960)

> The university started as a single community – a community of masters
> and students. It may even be said to have had a soul in the sense of
> a single animating principle. Today the large American university is,
> rather, a whole series of communities and activities held together by a
> common name, a common governing board, and related purposes. This
> great transformation is regretted by some, accepted by many, gloried in,
> as yet, by few. But it should be understood by all.   (Kerr, 1963)

These two quotations are from two of the many scholars who have taken on
from Newman the task of defining, or redefining, the idea of the university.
They point in rather different directions. Jaspers was reaffirming, in quasi-
metaphysical style, the unity of the university; Kerr pointed pragmatically to
the transatlantic future. This chapter does not attempt to join the debate at
any philosophical level. What I shall do is take up the notion of the university as a community, and explore the extent to which centrifugal pressures
make this notion increasingly inaccurate as an account of current practice,
and implausible as a view of the future.

Kerr's words of a quarter of a century ago have certainly been influential,
and the function and character of British higher education institutions have
been the subject of much scrutiny in the course of the expansion triggered by

the Robbins Report, published at exactly the time he was writing. Until recently, much of this concerned the extent to which the university can reserve its identity in the wake of substantial increases in student intake. The tension between élite and expansionist notions of higher education was the key theme of Halsey's further re-examination of the idea of a university (Halsey, 1985). He reviews contrasting historical notions of the university, drawing out the common theme of the institution as a community of science and learning but contrasting the different interpretations of its actual role. I suggest that there are material factors, some of quite recent origin, which in combination force a re-examination of the persistent notion of the university as a community. The most immediate and perhaps the most powerful of these is the change that has occurred in the nature of academic employment and the material circumstances of universities.

There is a rough analogy with the smashing of the physical atom. First, the analogy, like all analogies, provides no truths, only suggestive parallels whose quality is determined by their heuristic value, the extent to which they prompt thoughts and ideas which can then be developed and tested. Initially it suggests itself in two ways. First, the literal meaning of the atom – ατομοσ – is that it is indivisible. It cannot be cut. It is the irreducible core element of matter. We now know this to be true only etymologically; the atom itself (or rather the nucleus) has been smashed, and the concept of the irreducible core along with it. What, if anything, is irreducible about today's universities, or the elements that constitute them? The physical metaphor has been used before, for example by Lockwood (1987) in discussing the management of universities: 'The elementary particle of academic life is the individual faculty member, but the academic department is the primary unit in the structure.' But the analogy has not, to my knowledge, been pursued with reference to radical change in the make-up of the elements, nor in any detailed analysis of their relationships with each other.

Secondly, the smashing of the atom has released enormous amounts of energy. Some of this energy is controlled and has been used in positive ways, but there are major questions, still very much unresolved, about the uses and the dangers of the energy so created. The same may be true of the smashing of the academic atom: it is releasing considerable amounts of energy previously trapped within the confines of the institution, but the potential costs of the release have been only very hazily assessed.

The academic labour force: a community of equals?

The notion that members of the academic community exist on more or less equal terms is surely important to its presentation of itself as an academic community. Scott (1984) refers to the 'surprising solidarity' of British universities:

> The symptoms of this academic solidarity are a considerable equality of
> privileges and influence between senior and junior staff, the lack of any

significant division of labour between teachers and researchers, the absence of any serious stratification of institutions, and a remarkable homogeneity of intellectual and broader cultural values within the profession.

I want first to point to the increasing differentiation of academic labour; some of the other points will be taken up later.

There is a substantial debate within industrial sociology over the existence and significance of core and peripheral labour forces. Some argue that the labour force is increasingly divided between a core of permanent, relatively well-paid employees with security and career prospects, and a periphery of marginal workers employed on a part-time or temporary basis with little or no discernible occupational career. Others deny that this is in any way a new phenomenon, or argue that the proponents of the core-periphery thesis are in fact putting forward a model for managerial behaviour rather than an analysis of actual trends (see, for example, Atkinson and Meager, 1986; Pollert, 1987). Whatever the circumstances of industry generally, it is clear that there has been a significant growth in the numbers of both part-time and temporary workers in UK universities (and in the numbers of those who are both part-time and temporary). Part-time staff have increased from 1738 in 1981–82 to 3243 in 1986–87; as a proportion of total UK academic staff, this represents an increase from 3.8 per cent to 6.5 per cent (UGC statistics 1986–87, Vol. 1, table 25). Research by the Institute of Manpower Studies shows that the contract workers have increased too, from 6010 in 1976 to 8223 in 1981 and 10,249 in 1984; as proportions of all full-time academic staff these figures represent 15 per cent, 19 per cent and 23 per cent, respectively (Varlaam, 1987). Their numbers have certainly grown further since then.

Methodologically, the simple notion of part-time work is becoming increasingly suspect, as it covers weekly hours ranging all the way up to 30 and beyond and actually overlaps with jobs officially designated as full time (Kahne, 1988). Similarly, contract work covers a range of types, from the shortest of short-term to quite extensive rolling contracts which fall only just short of permanence in their duration. Clearly, contract work is not a staging-post on the way to tenure: over 40 per cent of the IMS sample were aged between 30 and 49, and the average length of time which those on contract have spent in that position is increasing, with 40 per cent in their fourth or greater year of contract work.

It is impossible to decide on the basis of quantitative information alone how these figures relate to individual preferences. There is the perennial chicken-and-egg argument about whether parents actually prefer to work part time to combine employment with child-rearing responsibilities, or whether this is a function of discrimination against women in the labour market combined with the absence of adequate child-care provision. But the figures, especially those relating to contract work, make it increasingly difficult to sustain the notion that academic staff on the whole enjoy the same conditions of employment. Marginal cases are now a large minority. Even if we count as permanent those who are appointed to university positions post-ERA (and therefore without tenure in the traditional sense – whatever *that* meant) it is likely that the 'core' will continue to diminish in relation to the periphery. At what point does the supposed community turn into a small élite of conversationalists, flanked by substantial numbers of people whose talking is done in front of classes, as temporary teachers, or to the word processor as contract researchers always with short-term deadlines to meet? Time horizons crucially affect the character of academic intercourse.

There is a strong gender dimension to this. A disproportionate number of the periphery are female workers, excluded from the core because of career interruptions or other reasons often related to the sexual division of labour (I am dealing here only with academic staff, but of course the whole notion of the university as a community is highly Athenian; one in every two males employed in universities is an academic, compared with one in every 15 women). As important as the numbers of men and women in different employment categories is the style and ethos of universities; I shall return to this later.

The idea of an academic community rests not only on the majority of academics enjoying the same terms of employment; it rests also on their sharing the same reward system. This may seem like a crude intrusion of the material into intellectual values, but it is at least arguable that a sense of community within universities depends in some measure on people being rewarded on the same basis for doing the same thing, i.e. teaching and research. Subjects and disciplines are not, in themselves, graded, though there may be an unofficial pecking order between them, both nationally and within particular institutions. This notion is being rapidly dispelled by the introduction of differential pay scales, allowing extra payments to those who can command a higher price elsewhere. It is here that the cultural specificity of the argument becomes apparent. In the USA, differentials in response to market forces have been the norm for a long time, if not from the time universities were first established. But in the UK the erosion of common salary scales marks a further weakening of the common bonds. I am not making a judgement on this, merely observing its (putative) effect. The greater the variation in pay scales, and in the discretionary elements in salary and remuneration packages generally, the less support is given by individual material bonds to the notion of community. Academic solidarity may not reach its highest form in the sharing of terms and conditions, but the absence of communality in such matters may pervade other, more intellectual, aspects of life together.

There are other material issues to be considered which lead outwards into areas that concern both academic freedom and the notion of community. Consultancy work on an individual and collective basis is growing fast. In some areas, it is virtually obligatory, as well as being an attraction as a means of enhancing academic salaries. It would be an odd business school that deterred its members from undertaking consultancies. Mixed contracts are now common, with people employed partly as academic staff by a university and partly as a consultant with an outside industrial concern. I do not wish to rehearse the arguments surrounding consultancy and contract work in general. Its relevance here is twofold.

First, it raises the issue of control and autonomy, with interesting questions such as how one decides the point at which control of a department, unit or even institution passes to the source of financial income (the sponsor); is it, for example, when critical analysis of its activities becomes practically difficult? – and how in turn is that to be assessed? Amy Guttman draws out well the difficulty of keeping in balance the individual and collective interests within the community:

> The more common and complex problem lies not in the influence that a particular consulting contract has on the integrity of one scholar's work, but in the way in which the widespread acceptance of consulting contracts can skew the types of problems that scholars pursue – drawing them away from more serious problems that have fewer immediate pay-offs or away from equally serious problems that afflict people who cannot afford to hire consultants. Not all types of research contracts interfere with the collective autonomy of scholarship, but many do. The more freedom that contracts give scholars to define their own research problems, the less they interfere with the collective autonomy of scholarship, which provides an intellectual sanctuary against political control of the creation of ideas. (Guttman, 1987)

Secondly, the management of consultancy and contracts directs attention towards internal relationships and stresses within universities. The growth of external income and its necessarily uneven distribution across departments or faculties adds inexorably to centrifugal pressures, as the departments with actual or potential earning power seek some 'return' on the revenue they are generating and/or seek to direct resources to enable them to increase that power. Internal fiscal policy may do something to maintain institutional identity, but the legitimacy of whatever formulae are constructed for these purposes must come under increasing strain (Richardson, 1991). The more explicit and understood the policy – if there is such – becomes, the more individual anomalies or feelings of unfairness are likely to emerge. It is not inconceivable that with a different general ethos, income-generating activities could contribute to rather than detract from a sense of common purpose within a university. But it would require a substantial shift for most people, and a shift too in the prevailing conceptions of what academic work is.

These material matters bring fresh salience to issues that have long been current in the long-running debate over the ends and values of the university. Defending himself against the criticisms of F.R. Leavis in 1970, Noel (now Lord) Annan wrote:

> One sometimes wonders whether Dr Leavis, who has spent his life in a university, has ever ... asked himself why it is that an academic community behaves in the way it does. Not only are dons asked to fulfil many more roles than they were a generation ago and, therefore,

find themselves committed to a multitude of new obligations. The conflict of these ends, many of which are good, is paralleled by the conflict – if they are humanists – in their work. They have to preserve and transmit the culture of the past, yet they are expected to break this golden bowl by their own innovations and discoveries. This conflict of roles and ends among the academic staff is echoed in the conflict of ends in the institution. Universities have always been vocational in their curricula. Many of their dons and students cannot avoid becoming entangled with industry, the health service and government itself. Yet at the same time some dons and students are bound to believe that above all they have a duty to proclaim ideals which are strongly opposed to the conventional wisdom of society.

(Annan, 1970)

Annan identifies the tension and implies that it is of value because it reflects, even enhances, the creative tension inherent in good academic work. A rather different view is offered by Squires, though he refers not to direct links with industry but to the growing professionalism of the curriculum. Given British attitudes to industry and the professions, one might have thought that the influence of the latter would be more welcome within higher education. But Squires observes:

Each course and each department is justified in terms of its own profession, academic or external, and there is therefore no general, institutional rationale. In fact, universities, polytechnics and colleges are largely administrative rather than academic entities; whereas the department embodies the discipline or field the institution as a whole embodies nothing – it is a curious mixture of bureaucracy and ritual.

(Squires, 1987)

But does the department embody the discipline? Squires suggests that it is at this level that the fundamental building-block of academic life is to be found. Yet others argue that departments are no longer intellectually coherent units in the way this suggests. Specialization in particular has dissolved the intellectual and other unity of departments, so that individuals look outside their department, and outside their institution altogether, for intellectual partnership (Becher, 1987). In further education, Tansley (1989) sees the course team as the new building block of college and curriculum organization drawing staff from a range of departments and forming a new locus of professional identity. *A Fragmented View* (FEU, 1986) records the diverse networks and patterns of identity, responsibility and accountability with which academic staff in FE feel themselves involved both internally and external to the institution.

It may be that the ideal of intellectual partnership based on common membership of a defined discipline within a wider community has always been exaggerated. Yet there can be little doubt that the shift identified by Scott (1984), from knowledge as process to knowledge as product, has had its effect, within a new configuration of relationships within universities, and between them and the state and other agents. Halsey sums it up thus:

> The university is more fissiparous, less integrated, more eager to respond to external influences, less separate from the mainstream of profane life, and therefore more serviceable as well as more pliant to the power of the state.   (Halsey, 1985)

Scott characterizes the modern university as increasingly a shared bureaucratic environment rather than an organic academic society (1984). The relationship between academic and administrative staff requires brief mention. There is, arguably, a redivision of labour here, as there has been within the academic staff itself. There has been a growth in the bureaucratic function within higher education, signalled on the one hand by increased numbers of administrative staff and on the other by an increased assumption of managerial roles by academic staff. Administrators themselves form a powerful sub-community within many institutions. How far are they regarded as an integral part of the original community, and what are the implications for internal academic relations? Whatever the quality of the relations, it can hardly be denied that their complexity has increased, giving universities still more of the character of a modern bureaucratic organization.

We are faced with increasing strains on academic loyalty, whatever that may be. Is the academic's prime loyalty to her or his students? To the department? To the institution? To the 'academic community'? To a sponsor? Or to him – or herself? It is perhaps unnecessary to talk in terms of prime loyalties; what we are trying to trace are the shifts in the balance of loyalties, especially those shifts that are sufficient to represent a dislocation of current focus. The pressure here is not simply a function of the growth and fragmentation of knowledge, which would anyway have exercised centrifugal pressure in a time of expansion or consolidation. It arises much more immediately from the fierce competition for resources at several different levels. These range from individuals competing against each other for research grants or academic posts, to departments or institutions competing for contracts of various kinds, to different parts of the post-secondary system competing for students. One consequence of this intensified competition, and the context within which it has been created, is what might be called, not too unhappily, the commodification of academic relations.

Expressed in its simplest form, this means the intrusion into university relationships, individual and collective, of an approach which calculates everything in terms of the resource implications. The implications may be directly financial; or, more commonly, of time, with consequences for output. At the most basic and yet very revealing level, this is illustrated in the reluctance of academics to attend meetings or seminars which are not directly relevant to their own field. The evidence for this is anecdotal, but the anecdotes are many. The notion of a departmental seminar which all members of the department regularly attend even if the topic is not one of immediate concern to them is almost obsolete in many faculties. There can

be few more telling signs of the break-up of a community than when participants so calculate the worth of an exchange that it must bring them the
promise of visible return before they enter into it. If the hour in the seminar
will not help them in their next article to be published — if it is only to hear
someone else expound their views and to offer a response — why bother to
attend?

The commodification of academic relations may be expressed in other
ways. Teaching and supervising students from other departments or contributing occasionally to courses run by colleagues in the same department
becomes more a matter of calculation as external pressures increase. The free
flow of ideas, inherent in the notion of an academic community, is threatened
by a climate which encourages the jealous guarding of original thoughts and
researchable propositions. The problems of safeguarding intellectual property rights assume new proportions. The extent of this is largely a matter of
conjecture at present. It rarely emerges in the crude form I have given to it
just now. Nor, it should be added, is it necessarily a bad thing for academics
to have to think about how they spend their time, and whether it is usefully
allocated to meetings to which they may have nothing to contribute and in
which they may have no substantive interest. But there is arguably a trend
towards rendering explicit — and thereby fundamentally altering the nature
of — the implicit contract of academic exchange which in its community form
involves interdependence and a willingness to contribute without visible and
direct return. The shift is away from a collective web towards a network of
individualized, bilateral and monetarized relationships.

In this section I have suggested that the relationship between the nucleus
of the community and its peripheral elements — the electrons, as it were — has
changed significantly, enough to provoke reconsideration of the structure of
the atom as a whole. I turn now to look more closely at some of the con-
stituent elements of the atom.

The irreducible core?

I come now to the question of the elements which must be present for a
university to retain an identity as an academic community. 'Presence' in this
context has two senses: the first refers to the existence within the institution
of certain academic components, without which it cannot be properly be
called a university; the second refers to the quality and quantity of the
physical presence of the people who make up the academic community and
give it its identity.

The various recent moves towards rationalization have prompted renewed
discussion along the lines 'when does a university cease to be a university?'
Halsey quotes Samuel Johnson's dictionary definition of a university as
'a school where *all* arts and faculties are taught' (my emphasis). In his discussion of academic freedom, O'Hear (1988) claims that 'a university without

the disciplines of history, literature and philosophy cannot be a university, however prestigious an institution it may be'. He refers to disciplines rather than departments, but the same argument has been deployed in defence of threatened departments of the last of the three in particular. By contrast, Keith Thomas (1988) has called for a re-examination of the rationale for the study of humanities in universities, and suggests that even a redrawing of disciplinary boundaries will not be enough to give it a convincing justification. In raising such an issue he makes explicit the need for subjects which were hitherto regarded as integral to a university to make a case for themselves. Previous assumptions about indispensability no longer hold.

It is not only subject but function that comes into question. The issue of what activities are indispensable to a university *qua* university has been given further prominence by the proposals to stratify universities into three grades, X, R and T. These would run directly against Scott's observation quoted earlier in this paper by distinguishing at institutional level between teaching and research. The point is not so much whether an institution engaged solely in teaching can legitimately be called a university. It is simply that the proposal itself, even if it is not implemented, both reflects and reinforces the pressure that is building up for further differentiation within the system. The designation of current polytechnics as universities, abolishing the structural differentiation of the binary line, will add further to this pressure by extending the usage of the term 'university' to institutions with a balance of activities very different from the current university norm, and a set of values deriving from different traditions (Stubbs, 1991).

Our prime concern is with the institution rather than the system, the atom rather than the body as a whole. The notion of the university as a community is often justified by reference to the span of its intellectual activities. Its wholeness derives from the breadth of disciplines which it covers. Communities may exist, but they are lacking the distinctive characteristic of a university community if there is not present somewhere on the campus a group flying the humanities flag, or doing science, or psychologizing. The assumption behind this must be that there is some interchange between these different disciplines, some osmotic process which goes beyond the mere fact that it brings together students who are taking different subjects.

Specialization has already dealt this image a succession of heavy blows; that has been widely commented upon in reviews of the development of knowledge and research. How far can departments genuinely claim to cover the entire field in which they are working, when specialties and subspecialties are proliferating at such a rate? If they cannot claim to be covering the field, is then the claim that, for example, philosophy is a *sine qua non* of university status reduced to the claim that there must be some representation of some branch of philosophy, however minimal? This would be a severe dilution of the original position.

Such arguments, themselves philosophical, have been usefully supplemented empirically by Tight's analysis of institutional characteristics, using

data supplied by universities and polytechnics (Tight, 1988). What this
shows is that only science and social studies have a significant presence in all
universities, though the latter dips to less than 9 per cent of the students in at
least one case. Engineering is present in all, but appears in one case to have
literally a minimal presence, studied by less than 1 per cent of the student
population. In other words, the notion that all universities (and polytechnics,
for that matter) include a basic core of subject areas does not seem to stand
up to scrutiny – unless, of course, one wanted to define the list of basic
subjects in order to allow this to occur.

We should also note here the stipulations proposed in 1988 by the University Grants Committee on the minimum viable size for physics and
chemistry departments, of 20 staff and 200 students. It certainly seems
sensible to suggest, on economic grounds, minimum sizes for subjects where
expensive technology is required, but can they sensibly be specified for other
subjects, on the basis that the subject is not properly covered without a
certain range of staff equipped to teach different specialities? The answer
may be yes, but imagine an exercise that gathered responses from different
departments in the same subject area across the country in respect of the
essential elements of their particular subject and therefore the minimum size
of their departments. In all probability, the standard deviation would be
quite high. As the *Times Higher Education Supplement* observed (30 September
1988):

> For all the talk of the importance of 'critical mass' in science there is
> little good evidence to back such a figure, or any other. And there is no
> convincing analysis of how the critical mass might vary over time, or
> within or between disciplines.

Yet this line of argument, although it may be useful in resisting a rigid
uniform approach to rationalization, has wider implications for the overall
coherence of the university, since if we know nothing about the impact of
such factors as size on academic quality this must cast doubt on many of the
proud pronouncements defending minimum subject groupings.

The second type of presence required is that of people. I used earlier the
curious notions of quantity and quality of presence. By quantity I mean how
often staff are present. To raise this is not to offer a clichéd jibe at academic
work habits. I refer instead to the financial pressures which are already
requiring serious scrutiny of the use of university premises. What is the
'capacity utilization' of most academic offices? What is the cost of providing
space for staff to work on campus during holidays? The growth of part-time
staff referred to above merely accentuates the issue. In cities where office costs
are extremely high, notably London, the cost of accommodating staff is a
major element in university budgets. Travel costs are high for the individual
where the imbalanced housing market has made it difficult for staff to live
reasonably near their work. Foreseeably – and here we move into the realm
of speculation to a large extent – there will be intensified use of offices, more

sharing, perhaps even time sharing; an office is Dr X's from Monday to Wednesday, Mr Y's on Thursday and Friday, and available as a seminar room for conferences at the weekends. Lectures and tutorials still have to be given. But when Rank Xerox calculates that it has been spending £3000 on overheads at its London office for each £1000 on salaries, and therefore launches its network scheme, converting senior and middle-level managers into self-employed consultants with a guarantee of a minimum amount of work from the company (Shirley, 1987), it is not inconceivable that universities will come to rethink the physical deployment of their staff. One strategy will be to reduce the amount of time that they are expected – or entitled – to spend on campus. New technology, in the shape of teleconferencing and so on, could facilitate this in the literal sense of making it easier, with no necessary implication as to the effect of such a move on the quality of teaching or research. It can be argued, indeed, that teleconferencing makes 'pure' academic communion easier, by removing the strains of personal face-to-face relationships.

Whether or not the quantity of staff presence is reduced in this way to a significant extent, the quality of people's presence is surely changing. The interstices of academic time, in which all kinds of intellectual plants – and weeds – grow, are being filled up. This may be a polite way of saying that academics now have to work harder and have less free time. We are in one sense back to the debate about what constitutes academic work – the ideas-in-the-bath phenomenon. If, as is mooted, the government is to carry out another diary exercise analysing the way academics spend their time, this may shed some light on whether there has indeed been an intensification of effort. Once again I am offering no judgement on how far this has been beneficial or the reverse. But the notion of the university as a community depends to an extent on corridor, if not common room, conversations, which occur on an unscheduled basis. That requires a degree of 'free' time. If academics become, as it were, employed on an internal consultancy basis, recruited to do a specified amount of teaching or research, there will be no space or time for the casual interchange which glues the academic enterprise together. Substantial condensation of atomic matter could have as much of an effect on its structure and character as the centrifugal forces I described earlier.

Such a scenario is recognizable as the Taylorisation of academic work, with the intensification of the use of university capital, human and physical. Presented in this stark and very sketchy way, it would appear to the majority of those affected a rather grim prospect. Yet it is unlikely that the patterns of academic work can remain static. As with industrial change in other sectors it will be a question of how notions such as efficiency and effectiveness are defined, and by whom (Schuller, 1991). Whatever the level of fragmentation and the accompanying reshaping of power relationships, it is hard to see the original idea of the university as a working community being sustained unchanged.

Concluding note: continuing education and the academic atom

Continuing education has a particular role to play in the changing nature of the academic community. By its very nature it increases the diversity of university activity in a number of ways. In so doing it increases the centrifugal forces at work. But it also illustrates how the energy released by the smashing of the academic atom may be turned to positive ends.

Its diversifying impact can be summarily presented (Duke, 1987). In varying degrees, continuing education leads first to a greater diversity within the student population. Academics are no longer teaching students of the same degree of homogeneity as they used to. On the one hand more 'non-tradional' groups are finding their way on to regular courses; on the other, new types of provision attract students from unfamiliar sources. So the student profile changes, as does the nature of what is being taught. Course structures become more diverse, and the steady rhythm of the traditional academic year becomes punctuated and disturbed by a whole range of short courses. Lecturing and tutorial work has to be supplemented by other teaching approaches, and supported by changes in the way admissions are handled and assessment is carried out, with more extensive counselling and guidance.

All of this demands new skills from the academic body (Schuller *et al.*, 1988). It means that collectively and individually academics are likely to find themselves doing a wider range of things. Not only are they not teaching the same subject as their colleagues, they are not even doing the same kind of thing. It is true that the young student engaged on a full-time degree is still the dominant student type. Arguably, the full-time degree is the basic bonding mechanism for the academic atom as it currently exists; if that is dethroned, dissolution is imminent. But even under the current system, enough change is taking place in both the population of universities and in their activities to erode in large measure the notion that they are composed of people of whom the designation student or staff member is enough to give a close account of what they actually do. Continuing education thus accelerates the redivision of academic labour and accentuates the diversification of individual and institutional role. It entails closer links with the local community. None of this makes the notion of the university as a community in itself impossible or invalid; but it does suggest a rethinking of how this is to be sustained.

I have argued that the university is subject to a range of forces which may effectively dissolve its claim to be a community in the sense of a unit with an internal cohesion and inherent bonding force. Whether it ever was is of course open to question. In the days of bachelors living in Oxbridge colleges, the sense was presumably a strong one. In this aspect, an equivalent historical change may have occurred when dons were allowed to marry and live out of college with their families, which must have radically changed the nature of academic life. Redbrick universities would never have had such an enclosed notion of the community, with the mutual embrace of university and local industry. Rich (1975) has argued that the university has in any case been a lopsided community; reviewing some accounts of how to 'make it' in academic life she concludes: 'What stands out is not the passion for "learning for its own sake" or the sense of intellectual community, but the dominance of the masculine ideal, the race of men against one another, the conversion of an end to a means.'

But whatever the strength of the original ideal and its actual embodiment, there are significant new pressures developing which will signal a quantum shift in the nature of the institution. Its break-up as a community in the existing sense may have painful consequences for some of those involved, and if handled wrongly may cause severe damage to the intellectual and educational life of the country more generally. Properly channelled, the energy released could nevertheless bring fresh vigour.

In his account of the discovery and development of nuclear energy, Patterson (1983) observes: 'It is worth stressing, some 40 years later, that the first to recognize the dilemma of nuclear energy – the conflict between its constructive and its destructive potentials – were the nuclear scientists themselves.' The question here is whether academics will similarly be the first to recognize what is happening and to explore the implications coolly. Their freedom to explore such an issue, and the habit of critical enquiry to which they aspire, should enable them to do so. If they do not, one consequence may be a reinterpretation, by others, of that very freedom.

Note

1. This is a slightly amended version of an article that first appeared in *Oxford Review of Education*, Vol. 16, No. 1, 1990. Permission to reproduce it here is gratefully acknowledged.

4

The Polytechnics

Jennifer Bone

From Robbins to the Education Reform Act

The announcement in the 1966 Government White Paper that 'The Government believes that the best results will be achieved by developing higher education on polytechnic lines wherever practicable' (DES, 1966), was put into effect initially in an atmosphere which, if not characterized by enthusiastic consensus, was at least relatively free of conflict. The consultations which had both preceded and followed Anthony Crosland's Woolwich speech, which pointed to the development of the 'binary' system, ensured a positive climate for the development of the newly designated institutions. Their work was to be distinguished by its comprehensive range and character, encompassing sub-degree and part-time provision alongside full-time and sandwich courses, and permitting communities of full-time and part-time staff with 'closer and more direct links with industry, business and the professions' (DES, 1966). Regional factors would influence their designation.

This new development within higher education fell within the orbit of the aims and principles set out in the 1963 Robbins Report, which still retain their influence. The reference to increased integration with the employer community predisposed the polytechnics towards the first of the aims enunciated by Robbins, namely 'instruction in skills suitable to play a part in the general division of labour' (Robbins, 1963). The 1972 White Paper (DES, 1972) *Education: A Framework for Expansion*, also acknowledged the importance of the employment factor, but explicitly declined to limit the value of higher education to such consideration; the polytechnics were thus entitled to set their expansion broadly within the entire Robbins philosophy.

There is now widespread recognition of the success of that expansion, both quantitatively and qualitatively. In recent years in particular, Polytechnics have experienced continuous growth when the universities have remained relatively static, and they have done so without a commensurate increase in resourcing (DES, 1989a). Moreover, the evidence does not bear out the frequent allegation that polytechnics have been tempted to drift academically in the direction of becoming quasi-universities, if this implies that they have departed from the characteristic goals defined at their establishment. A third of their students study part time and over a quarter for awards other than first and higher degrees (PCFC, 1990). Approximately a fifth of students follow sandwich courses which rely upon links with the employer community and a third of all students are over 25 years of age (DES, 1989a). Although they are national institutions, approximately a quarter of their students are recruited locally. Internally, the formative development of polytechnics was assisted by a widely shared educational vision, even if it stopped short of a philosophy, common to both management and unions. There was a fair degree of consensus on goals and targets which sustained the inevitable differences of view on ways and means. Polytechnics developed a strong sense of self-identity and the confidence that goes with it.

Before past achievement is read as a guarantee of future success, however, it would be prudent to note the extent to which circumstances favoured polytechnics. At their inception and in their early years, all significant interest groups supported or at least did not oppose their development. The only exceptions of any size were the colleges of teacher education who watched the polytechnic star wax as their own waned, but had no power base from which to prevent it. There was a secure bi-partisan political approach; their designation met the DES's wish for the creation of a coherent and cheaper sector of higher education outside the universities, and neatly accommodated the run-down of teacher education and the re-distribution of surplus staff and plant. It met the aspirations of the advanced technical sector of education and the determination of local education authorities that the next generation of institutions should not go the way of the former Colleges of Advanced Technology and slip from their grasp into the university sector. The universities had no sustained reasons for opposing the development. Only their departments of education were alarmed. Many senates had wearied of the tedium of establishing B.Ed degrees. They were not receptive to calls in the James Report (1972) to validate diversified degrees and were unenthusiastic about the proposed new Dip HE qualification. All this was much better left to the Council for National Academic Awards (CNAA).

This scenario of polytechnic success as a consequence of compatible self-interest in a context of convenient growth, rather than the realization of an educational consensus derived from strategic and synoptic planning, sufficed into the late eighties. It survived the continuing search for a planning machinery for public sector higher education which allowed central and local government joint control of academic rationalization and financial planning and the growing irritation within polytechnics at their answerability to a battery of outside bodies with the power to impinge upon their work and interfere with the exercise of their judgement. When the political consensus on public sector higher education broke and it became part of the larger conflict between central and local government, the outcome enshrined in the Education Reform Act coincided with the aspiration of the Committee of

Directors of Polytechnics (CDP) and was probably welcome to a goodly proportion of staff, whatever the reservations of the major union. Polytechnics became autonomous self-governing institutions with the financial status of higher education corporations.

The changed status of the polytechnics has been accompanied by warm commendations from government and elsewhere of their course and student profiles, their management style and their cost effectiveness. The White Paper, *Higher Education: Meeting the Challenge* (DES, 1987), which preceded the publication of the Education Reform Bill, gave the obligatory nod in the direction of Robbins' four aims but then unashamedly concentrated upon the first aim in the interests of the national economy, territory that the polytechnics understandably regard as distinctively theirs. The advocacy from a number of influential quarters of flexibility in course design, modes of study, modularity, and opportunity for credit transfer in both initial and continuing education, coupled with the need to give full credence to vocational qualifications and appropriate work experience as a proper preparation for higher education, fits well with the polytechnics' track record and their mission statements. The Chairman of the PCFC, who will also chair the English Higher Education Funding Council (HEFC) has expressed his confidence that the sector is in a 'long-term growth market' and should actively promote what it offers to a public which does not yet give it full value (Dearing, 1989). It is understandable if polytechnics are tempted to claim that higher education's agenda for the next decade is their agenda and that they are uniquely qualified to deliver it.

Innovation in the form and content of higher education within polytechnics has been developed within a financial regime and an educational ethos which still presume the Robbins formula. Trow argues that whatever the distinctive character intended for polytechnics, they had to meet and be funded to meet the expectations derived from Robbins to establish their legitimacy as higher education institutions. The values and assumptions of Robbins are:

> still the defining characteristics of British higher education, with little fundamental change over the past quarter century as the numbers have increased fourfold. And that is why Robbins was a trap, because it promised growth, without creating the structural and normative conditions for continued growth and development towards mass higher education.   (Trow, 1989)

Trow's judgement implies that the *sine qua non* for the realization of polytechnic credibility was the demonstration that their degree and postgraduate level work is commensurate with the generally accepted norms of university provision. The Charter of the Council for National Academic Awards required it; and the Council can take its share of the credit for the outcome. Polytechnic staff whose own education and, frequently, former work experience had familiarized them with the conventions of university practice were only too anxious to provide courses of at least an equivalent quality, while having to recognize the limitations of disparity in resources, both historically accumulated and upheld by recurrent funding. They have done so in subject areas and fields of study difficult to equate with classical university provision and using a more varied assessment methodology than has been associated historically with university education. There has been an enormous investment of energy and endeavour to meet the prescribed canons of quality control and quality assurance. It is clear that the polytechnic experience has had repercussions for university approaches to the measurement and demonstration of quality and it is not beyond the bounds of possibility that there can be some fruitful cooperation across the binary line. Degree awarding powers for polytechnics are the essential prerequisite.

It would be ironic, however, if the polytechnics' success in playing by the Robbins rules proves to have undermined their capacity to spearhead the breakthrough to mass higher education which is now so urgently needed and on which, in principle, they should be well placed to give a lead. *More Means Different* (Ball, 1990) challenged higher education to sacrifice its sacred cows including the dominant place of the three-year full-time degree, the three term year, and the assumption that teaching and research are inseparable. In short, higher education needs to reconsider its presumptions about quality and excellence, and how they are to be evaluated, as its necessary contribution to the national campaign called for in that report to raise awareness of the economic, social and personal return from advanced education and training. For a polytechnic sector that has devoted much effort to establishing parity with universities by conventional standards, it is a challenging and contentious belief.

Prospects for continuing expansion

A belief in the desirability of continuing the expansion of higher education is, for all practical purposes, universal. Age participation rates of 25 or 30 per cent are being canvassed in some quarters. Central policy and planning, however, continue to be based on an incremental approach, while a philosophy of mass higher education is, at best, in its infancy. The nub of the issue has been trenchantly expressed by Peter Scott. Having noted that 1990 may be seen in retrospect as the start of the post-binary era, he continued:

> 1990 may also be remembered as the year in which Britain began to move towards a mass-access system as well, irreversibly and irresolutely – irreversibly because almost everyone now accepts that further substantial expansion is inevitable and almost no-one argues for the maintenance of a selective, elitist system: irresolutely, because instead of confronting the primary questions about the scale, structure and mission of a mass system, policy makers have confined their attention to the essentially secondary issue of 'who pays?' (Scott, 1990)

When subject to analysis, the consensus in support of expansion may thus prove more apparent than real. It includes a number of different ideological approaches and potentially conflicting interests. The dominant factor is the predicted need of the national economy, but mingled with it are concepts of expansion through value for money resulting from the application of commercially derived management approaches, financing the mass-access system as a simulated mass-market, and the shaping of the curriculum and of student experience of learning along lines which are more directly governed by employment considerations.

If the economic argument is paramount then agreement on the scale of national need and demand for higher education is a pre-requisite of planning. Agreement on education and training as 'essential components in generating what we might call national competence' (Yates, 1990) is readily available: witness the plethora of initiatives for closer links between higher education and industry, which have been actively pursued by polytechnics and others. The question remains whether progress with these measures to date may obscure the extent of the investment required to ensure UK competitiveness internationally and the nature of the cultural shift necessary to persuade the population at large that higher education is the entitlement of more than a privileged minority and that continuing education will be the norm for career and employment progress. It is widely argued that only an active tri-partite consensus of government, employers and higher education can bring about such expansion within measurable time. It has also been a constantly reiterated theme of consultation between industry and higher education that only government can properly fulfil the key conditions for securing the well-being of higher education and for combining expansion with the maintenance of quality.

These key conditions are as follows:

1. An adequate financial framework.
2. Provision of the necessary higher education capacity.
3. The adoption of a coordinated network of qualifications both to facilitate wider entry to higher education and to ensure a sufficient range of awards within it.

Trow's definition of the Robbins trap is based as much on the organization and structure of higher education as on its aims and the current gold standard of its awards. Proposals for 're-thinking Robbins' tend to be met with a suspicion that they are a cover for justifying further reductions in funding, or for providing less well qualified entrants with a restricted educational opportunity and a less valuable qualification on exit. Such suspicion is not wholly unjustified, but it should not obscure the crucial issue of whether a creative educational response to expansion can emerge from within the higher education system with sufficient force. It is unlikely to do so without a supportive national context; it is equally clear that hard thought and flexible approaches will be needed from the system itself.

Quality and funding

To place funding at the head of the list is to reflect the pre-occupation of the past decade. In the coming decade it will condition if not determine the scope for expansion. Growth in the 1980s was accommodated in the public sector with a diminishing unit of resource. With the establishment of PCFC and its funding methodology, the trend has been accelerated by the inevitable readiness of the heads of PCFC institutions, given the rules of the game, to bid competitively or face the prospect of managing a contracting institution with a declining income. This willingness to expand has not only been a consequence of financial necessity but also the implementation of a commitment to enlarging educational opportunity. The outcome has been seized upon by government ministers as evidence that 'public sector' higher education can continue to accommodate increased numbers, educated more cheaply, with no apparent loss in quality. To the claim of CDP/CVCP (1990) that the process cannot go on indefinitely, but that a balance must be struck between quality and price, the Secretary of State retorted, in a speech to the CDP Annual Conference:

> I was disappointed to read ... 'there is a balance to be struck between price and quality'. I know of no evidence which relates the two in the short term and at the margins, where you are operating. Indeed, I am advised that there is no correlation at all in the polytechnics between the prices bid for student numbers and HMI quality assessments ... It is common experience in other industries that increasing volume enables both higher quality and lower unit costs. What is different about yours?

The strenuous efforts successfully made to combine quality and expansion lend verisimilitude to the Secretary of State's argument, the more so as no individual institution has yet been prepared to give credence to the CDP/CVCP position by declaring that financial pressures are damaging its excellence. Yet changing staff: student ratios and more intensive use of plant and facilities cannot continue *ad infinitum* without substantially affecting the student's educational experience. Higher education in the UK has historically provided access to high grade library, computing and other facilities; space in which to study; a variety of forms of tuition and assessment (some of them very labour intensive); above all, time and opportunity for staff–student educational exchange through the medium of tutorial and more informal contact. In polytechnics, the limits of this approach are being reached.

There is no good reason why higher education should escape the obligation to demonstrate what its various activities cost, nor does it follow that a low-cost course, properly designed and taught to a tight budget, will not provide an education of quality. But if the unit of resource continues to diminish, institutions committed to sustaining quality could be forced to offer only a limited range of cheap-cost, high-demand courses, thus impoverishing the system, undermining regional provision and diminishing professional scope and job satisfaction for staff. Moreover, however cost effective they are, the more significant financial determinants of polytechnic futures are likely to include changes in student maintenance support, with its consequences for the convention of full-time higher education being undertaken away from home, loans, financial support for part-time study and tax incentives for continuing education. Nonetheless, the inevitability of differentiation of cheaper from higher cost courses will have to be addressed, and of critical concern to polytechnic staff will be the effect on institutional character, diversity and prestige.

Quality and institutional diversity

As far as the structure and capacity of higher education is concerned, the 1990s can be expected to be a decade of increasing institutional diversity. As Slee (1990) argued:

> Knowing how different you want to be and recognizing how different you have to be, will mark the distinction between leader and led. The leaders will already have defined their product and have begun marketing their brand image to employers, niche communities and government.

Some concentration of research capability now seems inevitable and the continuation of an increasingly élite tradition of undergraduate education in the conventional three-year residential mould in a limited number of places seems highly probable. For 2000 and beyond the scene is much more open. The present government has signalled its commitment to diversity of provision and urged institutions to play to their strengths, the Secretary of State indicating that in the case of polytechnics and colleges he regards this as 'concentrating on teaching and especially on vocational, professional and industrially based teaching courses at all levels of higher education. I see this as their collective mission' (MacGregor, 1990). The hazard of this commission is that it could result in the PCFC sector, spearheaded by the polytechnics, bearing the brunt of expansion alone, by having to provide only lower cost courses and perhaps shorter more intensive degrees, as the culminating point in a series of vocational qualifications which start at secondary school, are kitemarked by the National Council of Vocational Qualification (NCVQ) and directly open to employer influence and demand.

The point, however, is not whether the UK should maintain an élite strand both in research and in undergraduate teaching, but whether the majority of institutions will collectively provide a sufficiently integrated and flexible system to permit increased access, variety of study opportunity in both initial and continuing education and innovation in teaching and learning, combined with scope for institutions to play to their strengths, both professionally and scholastically. In these circumstances it would be legitimate to require them to provide at least a proportion of the education they offer very cheaply, and differential core funding could be adjusted from time to time to reinforce response to identified national need. But if there is to be genuine institutional choice towards expanding educational opportunity then this must be reflected in equality in public funding and in institutional responsibility for quality.

If, in the event, the scale of institutional change in the 1990s proves to be incremental rather than explosive, polytechnics as a group can expect to hold their own. Either way, safeguarding quality will remain of first importance: no one is looking for poor quality higher education nor are the best representatives of employers seeking a narrow vocationalism at the expense of its wider purposes. 'Higher education as a national asset, must maintain its humane values and be strong in all its disciplines, while ensuring that the language and perspectives of mathematics, science and technology, essential for modern working life, are properly familiar to all those it educates' (CIHE, 1987).

The key guarantors of quality are the staff, and institutional management will need to place high priority on career opportunity and professional satisfaction which make it worthwhile for gifted individuals to entertain the idea of spending at least a proportion of their working lives within education. Improved mobility between education and other employment will be vital if higher education is to remain sufficiently in touch with developments beyond it. The range of expertise required of staff needs fuller recognition. The prestige that attaches to scholarship or research is necessary and secure; belated emphasis on the importance of teaching quality has not as yet been accompanied by adequate exploration or recognition of the skills and professionalism implicit in teaching excellence, or of the likely demands of meeting the needs of an enlarged constituency. Proper recognition of staff professionalism also has implications for institutional management. The efficient organization of academic life cannot necessarily be guaranteed by the application of a methodology applicable to commercial success. The intellectual and educational vitality of an academic community is dependent upon cooperative interchange. In higher education 'the interrelationship of qualitative and quantitative factors in most decisions present continual value judgements to decision makers . . . as long as the key values remain, the essential nature of the academic institution will survive' (Fielden, 1990).

Quality and qualifications

A third condition for successful expansion is further exploration of the appropriate range of higher education qualifications and the ways in which different awards could be related to each other. The subject is necessarily complicated, having to take account of professional and vocational considerations as well as academic interests. Innovation in the direction of flexible modules of study and patterns of award, in both initial and continuing education, credit transfer, franchising, accreditation of in-company based education and training have become hallmarks of polytechnic mission and strategy and all are facilitating growth and widening access. The underlying question relates to the relative currency of different awards; if the charge of offering a reduced version of higher education is to be avoided, then reconsideration of qualifications needs to be accompanied by a more complete statement of the philosophy, purpose and value of such a transition than has so far been proposed. The defensiveness of the system in recent years has allowed the government to set the agenda and limit the debate. The lack of a comprehensive concern for purpose and value (for which higher education must itself bear the responsibility) has had its consequences in the 'nervous tinkering, ideological dreaming, political evasion and managerial bombast which passed for a vigorous higher education policy in 1990' (Scott, 1990). Wright suggests that it is now beginning to develop:

> there are some signs that the changing social and cultural environment is beginning to form new conceptions of education, quality and personal fulfilment . . . one might expect a different version of higher education to emerge in the late twentieth century world under the sway of powerful international currents and the dizzying growth of information techno-logy and communications.   (Wright, 1990)

Attention to these 'new conceptions of education' might go some way to avoid the sterility of argument between academic and applied emphases. In her vigorous defence of the university tradition, Mary Warnock (1989) pointed to the importance of students, through their teachers, 'standing on the edge of a developing and changing world of learning', the necessity, when knowledge so quickly dates, of an understanding of principles, and of the need to develop imagination as a proper concern of the democratic state. None of this is unfamiliar or uncomfortable ground for the approach to education developed in polytechnics and their starting point may shed fresh light on it. For understandable reasons, polytechnics have to date paid more attention to quality processes than to articulating the philosophy that under-lies them. One of the few systematic and useful contributions so far has been the analysis of an educational approach through process and problem solving (Birch, 1988); however, it is hard to avoid the conclusion that a sufficient philosophy of higher education must also grapple with issues inherent in the use, management and advancement of knowledge. The importance of higher education maintaining, as its social function, both 'receptiveness and detach-ment' (Meyer-Dohm, 1990) needs reinforcing if the next and enlarged gen-eration of students is not to be short changed.

Successful expansion will require vision as well as pragmatism. Post-Thatcher, there is no danger of a cosy consensus, rather every prospect of tension and conflict; but out of it might emerge the necessary creative cooperation and understanding. If the polytechnic sector can bring its dis-tinctive experience to bear in such debate, then whatever its future identity in any re-ordering of higher education, it will ensure its contribution to edu-cational advance in the coming decade.

5

Other Colleges

David Bradshaw

There is something slightly down-market, less pure than pure, about the expression 'other' colleges. It suggests after-thought, or bits and pieces left over. Yet it catches a common perception. We have universities and polytechnics and we have an amorphous unclassifiable remainder. *Polytechnics and Other Colleges*, the title of a 1966 White Paper (DES, 1966) reflected this quality and the lack of a simply stated inclusive title. Twenty-five years later another White Paper *Higher Education: A New Framework* (HMSO, 1991c) cleared the way for polytechnics to be restyled universities but found it equally difficult to find an institutional title to embrace 'the diversity of other higher education institutions'. At the same time the sharp line drawn in the Education Reform Act of 1988 between institutions with more than 55 per cent of advanced work and colleges with less, had done nothing to prevent the growth of higher education in non-incorporated institutions teaching mainly further education courses.

There never has been a totally self-contained system of higher education, not least because educational systems reflect ways of distributing money, especially where power is divided between central and local government. So categories must be drawn up and definitions made and even the most sensitive are, in the end, arbitrary. As a result there have always been colleges that fail to meet the administrative critieria for recognition as institutions of higher education; colleges that are specialist (in, say, Dance or Agriculture); colleges with a mixture of work, not all of which is 'advanced' or 'higher'; and colleges that have broken the mould of preconceptions as to what colleges should be like. Other countries draw distinctions but in a different place. Institutions in the USA include much within their higher education curricula in terms of knowledge, concepts and intellectual demand which in the UK is studied at GCE Advanced or BTEC National levels. But any system tends to reinforce its own distinctions, once it has introduced them. 'Other colleges' may lack precision and status but it is also a warmly inclusive term, its ambiguity is open and admissive; where nothing is ruled in, nothing is ruled out.

As funded today other colleges include just a few specialist monotechnic colleges such as the Rose Bruford College of Speech and Drama (187 students in 1987–88) and the North Riding College (one of the very few remaining monotechnic teacher training institutions). These are survivors which have remained free standing for reasons of geography and their own ability to win, politically, the argument for independence. (I had originally included the Camborne School of Mines with just over 200 students in my examples. In November 1991 its merger with the University of Exeter was announced.) But most colleges, either by choice or the result of external pressure, are now cast in the contemporary mould of conglomerates. These multi-purpose institutions represent two lines of development in particular. One is the growth of courses, especially in the humanities and social sciences in the former colleges of education; the other is the tradition of further education. The first came from an unexpected windfall of places made available when the expansion of teacher training colleges in the 1960s, a response to the baby boom, resulted in massive over-provision when there was an unpredicted and very sharp decline in the birth rate. The second represents a long-standing tradition in which successive governments have used FE colleges which have developed their more advanced work as the base to develop new institutions of higher education. In England and Wales ten colleges of technology became Colleges of Advanced Technology in the late 1950s and within a few years received their charters to become universities. A decade later the colleges of FE provided another much larger number to become the 30 polytechnics in England and Wales, also now to be universities.

More recently others again singly or in combination with one another or with former colleges of education became colleges and institutes of *higher* education. In general where further education colleges were part of the new institutions, they tended to become like polytechnics, though somewhat smaller in size. Where they are built upon colleges of education alone they have a distinctiveness of style and often of curriculum.

The same underlying forces, such as demographic factors and political perceptions of the gross national requirement for higher education, have been at work in both Scotland and Northern Ireland, and much higher education there has also been developed within the colleges of further education. So much of the development in those two countries has followed similar patterns to the rest of the UK and their stories illustrate the same blend of carefully enunciated principle implemented with healthy pragmatism. But there have been some significant differences in the detail of development.

In Scotland central government has funded most higher education outside of the universities since early in the century, and has included institutions ranging from broad-based colleges (such as Paisley College of Technology and Robert Gordon's College, Aberdeen) to specialist colleges of education and agriculture. But local government (in Scotland based upon regions) has been active too. In recent years the plans to form Heriot-Watt University in Edinburgh and the University of Strathclyde in Glasgow both involved the development of existing institutions. As plans advanced, local government established Glasgow and Napier Colleges as major civic institutions. At the end of the 1980s the funding of both was transferred from the regional councils to the Scottish Education Department. Both are now styled polytechnics, and will be universities in the near future.

In Northern Ireland, too, there have been a number of institutions offering what is now defined as further and higher education for some decades, and, as in England and Wales, the mix of levels has varied between one institution and another. Following the publication of the Lockwood Report in 1965 (Northern Ireland Ministry of Education, 1965), the government of Northern Ireland established the New University of Ulster and the Ulster College soon to be renamed the Ulster Polytechnic. Existing specialist Colleges of Art and Home Economics along with some Teacher Education were brought into the Polytechnic and much Advanced Further Education was transferred into it from colleges of further education. Even so much of the development was new. The New University of Ulster had some difficulty in meeting its expansion targets and there was also an anomaly in that the Department of Education, Northern Ireland (DENI) was then funding directly two separate sectors of Higher Education. This was resolved when Ulster Polytechnic joined with the New University of Ulster, to establish the present University of Ulster with a new charter and statutes (DENI, 1982). These were unique in that they specifically allowed for the continuation of BTEC validated work in the University. A few colleges of further education have subsequently regained some higher education courses, especially BTEC Higher National courses.

But neither Scotland nor Northern Ireland has Colleges of Higher Education built upon former colleges of education and offering both teacher training and non-vocational courses. Several of the colleges of education were very large (Jordanhill, for example, had a student population of more than 3000 in the early 1970s) and the Scottish Education Department preferred to keep a few fairly large mono-technic institutions to the option of diversifying a larger number of colleges. There was also the complication that in Scotland many students enter the universities at the age of 17, a year before they could begin teacher training. This was thought likely to create difficulties for the colleges if they started to offer non-vocational BAs. In Northern Ireland the creation of additional non-vocational opportunities would have made the problems of the New University of Ulster worse, and again the colleges of education were of sufficient size to contract but remain viable as well as having political/denominational lobbies. So the 'other college' tradition in both countries lies in the further education tradition; there is no additional dimension as in England and Wales.

While the distribution of money provides perhaps the most important part of the system's organizing framework the processes of examining and validation provide two others. Examination practice attempts to ensure comparability of standards, and with some examiners crossing the obsolescent binary line there is a thread of comparability across the whole system too. As to validation the CNAA and the Business and Technician Education Council

(BTEC) have been additional sources of coherence among institutions. However, some of the sense of coherence is now disappearing. Universities are almost by definition self-validating, and the powers latterly vested in polytechnics by the CNAA made them virtually so. This development, desirable though it may have been for the polytechnics, reduced the strength of common validation procedures in the public sector to provide a sense of community within it.

A further erosion will occur when the proposals in *Higher Education: A New Framework*, and subsequent legislation to wind up the CNAA are put into effect since institutions will have to depend upon other individual institutions for the validation of courses, so losing some of their capacity to act independently and some of their sense of being equal before the validators. It will replace one kind of boundary between institutions with another, and while franchising of courses from one institution to another has become commonplace and has increased the number of institutions in which degree-level work is taught, if it were to become the only way of extending such opportunities outside of the institutions with degree awarding powers it would have the effect of making a boundary between degree awarding and other colleges the sharper.

Until fairly recently traditions in British higher education were fairly specific to types of institution. A crudely simple summary would be that universities were largely research led and retained some belief in the value of residence for students, while technical colleges were employment led and had a particular concern to provide opportunities for people in employment (or, later, not) to study part-time. As higher education has come to be seen as an entity and the pressures upon universities to be more employment aware, and polytechnics to acknowledge the received view of the place of research in degree work have increased, so these distinctions have blurred. But they have not disappeared altogether.

The colleges of education brought other traditions. Freud and Jung had showed that the intellect could not be developed in isolation and Piaget that intellectual growth was in stages which had previously been neglected. These insights and others from the burgeoning output of psychologists, in the USA in particular, resulted in a concern to take account of how children learn and with it came new approaches not only to teaching children, but to teaching students also. It showed itself in the widespread use of teaching by discussion methods, student-led seminars and project work. There was also a concern to support students by active personal tutor systems, though students often found these less helpful than was intended in their foundation. Similar influences were at work in the university departments of education; but they had very little influence on what happened elsewhere in the universities. But the universities certainly influenced the colleges when the colleges developed strong main courses under university tutelage. For the students the aim was 'to carry further the personal development of the student . . . by taking one or more main subjects with the most mature approach and at the highest level of which they are capable', while the courses were to be 'of a standard nationally acceptable and a quality comparable with that of the universities' (Minis-try of Education, 1957).

University influence became even stronger after 1963 with the introduction of B.Ed courses. Many serving teachers thought the main courses and their heavy emphasis upon academic values an inappropriate preparation for work in the classroom. But for the subsequent development of the colleges it was certainly useful in establishing their credibility to teach at degree level. The colleges developed vigorously and often distinctively in the humanities, social sciences and many art forms. It was on this base that the colleges began their non-teacher training work when they were authorized (DES, 1974) to offer unit-based Dip HE and degree courses which drew on modules developed for B.Ed courses while remaining non-vocational in character. From them has grown the core of the work of this group of colleges. Life has not been easy for them. The lack of a vocational focus in their non-teacher training courses placed them outside the preferred lines of development as soon as national policy made vocational relevance the leading principle for change and growth, and a lack of resources has made the development of new work very difficult.

Their concern for individuals and their development brought one more major contribution from the colleges of education to higher education as a whole by opening up further opportunities for mature students. Adults have attended part-time in further education for many years and many thousands of ex-servicemen enrolled in the universities just after the war. Then in the late 1950s and early 1960s colleges of education extended these opportunities when, in response to an acute shortage of teachers, many colleges admitted some mature students, and following the example of Manchester which had opened a day college for mature students as early as 1950, a number of LEAs established colleges specifically for this group. While most part-timers in FE and ex-service students were men, now, for the first time, substantial num-bers of women came into higher education. Early fears that the pool of potential students was limited and that recruitment could not be maintained proved groundless. By the mid-1960s one student in seven in colleges of education was an adult. Women entered colleges after careers in business, clerical occupations or nursing, or in home-making and child rearing. There were men too, again from widely differing backgrounds. Many (men and women alike) lacked confidence, some needed special support during school holidays and sympathetic timetabling; but most did well and some were outstanding. Opportunities in the arts and social studies attracted them particularly since the prerequisites for entry, though real, were in the realm of intellectual skills, wide reading and dedication rather than in required specific knowledge as was often the case in the sciences or in mathematics.

Some of the colleges of education were also especially concerned to pro-vide students with a breadth of study to balance the specialism pursued in their main courses, and a growing number required students to pursue an interdisciplinary study of some kind. The institutes and colleges of higher education inherited these traditions in the 1970s and concern for the individual, breadth of experience and participative teaching methods, have characterized them since their foundation.

If governments saw little scope for expansion until the late 1980s, they did see substantial room for change and in particular for much greater emphasis on employment relevance and on the efficient use of resources. Both reflected changing public attitudes. The growing concern over the relevance of education, first articulated at cabinet level by James Callaghan in his Ruskin College speech, was pressed by Mrs Thatcher's first two administrations with sharp questions as to the purposes of education and preparation for employment in particular. The Callaghan Government similarly began the search for firmer control of costs, especially through the Oakes Report (DES, 1978) but again it was Mrs Thatcher's Governments that pursued the issues to reform when Sir Keith Joseph set up the National Advisory Body (NAB) as a new administrative instrument to handle higher education outside the universities. While its main concern was with planning and funding, it also had substantial influence on direction and purpose. And although only advisory in status, with the power of decision resting with the Secretary of State, NAB significantly changed the direction of higher education. The cost of the service overall was brought under firm control, and the per-capita expenditure on students reduced. Employment related programmes were extended, less obviously 'relevant' areas encouraged to develop employment awareness and such new money as was available was channelled into areas of great need like Information Technology.

NAB also used its position to extend opportunities for mature students and was far more even handed in its treatment of non-polytechnic colleges than the committee of regional staff inspectors had been. It argued persuasively for expansion and although acceptance of the need to make substantially greater provision was slow in coming the NAB helped to convince officials and politicians at the DES that it was needed.

During Mrs Thatcher's second term of office political thinking at the DES began to move in the direction of opening the whole of the education system to the influence of market forces. The applicability of these forces to education has been hotly debated; for this account the only significance is that it was attempted. The new thinking appeared in the 1987 White Paper, *Higher Education: Meeting the Challenge* (DES, 1987) which drew a clear line between institutions that were to become independent, incorporated institutions, and those colleges that were to remain within the local authority system. Thus in the ensuing Education Reform Act of 1988 the division between the mainstream of higher education and the 'other colleges' remained, but with the line between them drawn in a rather different place. The White Paper and the Act also provided for the balance of planning and competition in the distribution of funds to be shifted strongly towards the latter.

Simultaneously, there was the prospect of some modest expansion and this has grown into a realization that the higher education system does not contain enough places to provide the highly qualified people needed to enable Britain to compete effectively in the international market-place. After more than a century of neglect of vocationally oriented education, skill shortages at advanced levels are now seen as one of the main barriers to British penetration of the high value-added markets of the world. In the barren decade 1976–85 the possibility of over-provision of highly skilled people was an important consideration in the minds of senior civil servants. The current conviction is that much greater participation in the whole range of post-school opportunities is needed to develop a work-force that can cope with the current economic challenges. As a concomitant there is an urgent need to educate more of the mature population.

So the present system has emerged through many pressures – a mix of political necessity, administrative thinking (both characteristically constrained by short time-scales), institutional initiative or inertia, the pressures of educational tradition, the needs of employers and the preferences of students. The next ten years will be, if not dominated by, then at least much concerned with the continued tight control of the efficiency of the whole operation, the provision of highly qualified people for employment and awareness of such new concerns as environmental issues. But just as 'the past is a foreign country' where things are done differently, so also is the future. The danger is that in looking to the future we extrapolate too much of the structures of the past; the Robbins Report for all its vision and thoroughness did this. The future also will afford opportunity to think principles out anew, to attempt to solve problems both old and new in fresh ways. *More Means Different* (Ball, 1990) catches the need. Universities and polytechnics are changing rapidly and will change still further and so will the other colleges. But even during a time of rapid change traditions remain and though they, too, change over time, they change more slowly than structures, and even than the aims and objectives from which, ultimately, new traditions may stem.

With the Education Reform Act of 1988 many of yesterday's other colleges have become part of the undisputed mainstream of today, where they add something of their own traditions to the evolving generality. There is within the mainstream a hierarchy of institutions. With the appearance of proposals to accord the title of university to polytechnic institutions, and changes in validation procedures, public perceptions of hierarchy may change over the next few years, but the awareness of which institutions are in the mainstream is likely to remain. As, however, these changes come about a new group of 'other colleges' is emerging currently within local authorities (see Chapter 10). If the hopes for growth and change are to be realized they will be of some importance over the next decade. They will work within a fast altering context. The world economy is expected to continue its rapid change, and international competition to increase. The content of work will increasingly become intellectual: one estimate is that by the year 2000, 70 per cent of all the jobs in Europe will require cerebral rather than practical skills, though many jobs will require both. In consequence employment relevance will become even more important. This will affect not only the knowledge content of syllabuses but bring an increased emphasis on process.

Employers are already requiring more attention to the skills developed in higher education since it is these, rather than degree-course knowledge, which they use when they employ the majority of graduates. As they respond to this demand, teachers throughout higher education may find that by developing the process content of their courses they can also enhance their purely academic concerns. That these developments will affect all of their education is well illustrated from a redbrick university where a group of staff have set their objectives as, 'process not product; education for all; less examinations more project work; different methods of evaluation; a teaching and learning resource centre ... the university as a community resource' (Sheffield University, 1990).

There are other pressures against the system as a whole too. There are new pressures for higher education to balance its specialisms with recognition of the need for breadth, and with growing concern about the state of the world environment pressure to act (and in being educated to take account of) far tighter ecological constraints (as Gray, Chapter 6, recognizes for FE).

As governments and employers respond to these needs so people's expectations will change; we shall begin to become a 'learning society' in which the belief that a sound initial education can carry people through life is replaced by a belief that learning is one of life's permanent conditions, supported informally by experience of many kinds and also sustained by many agencies. So leaving school will become not an end to education but a transition to other kinds of learning, and a far higher proportion of the population will include higher education among their expectations. As higher education becomes the expectation first of more, and then of most of the population it may lose some of its mystique, but it will not lose its hierarchies. The universities, enlarged as a group when the polytechnics receive their charters, will probably retain most status followed by the major colleges of higher education, while the 'other colleges' may carry less prestige than either. For quite apart from the significance of title (still significant in the UK) hierarchies based on proportions of higher education within institutions, the presence of post-graduate courses and the power to validate or not to do so are likely to be seen as criteria of significant difference.

Government has created a system in which institutions compete with one another for resources and compete more than in the past for students. This can only be to the advantage of the institutions built upon former colleges of education since they have learned to live within the tightest of budget margins and will now be able to move into curriculum areas previously not available to them. But with their vocational orientation, their continuing responsiveness to local communities, and to part-time needs, their experience of developing access courses for previously under-represented groups and success in developing livelier methods of teaching, colleges of further education are even better placed to be prominent in the inevitable expansion. Part-time provision in many modes will be particularly important. For although the spread of car ownership makes geographical access less of a problem than it once was (and has contributed to the growth of part-time enrolments in polytechnics), 60 per cent of households still have no car and 60 per cent of women do not hold a driving licence. So there are still many for whom proximity of opportunity decides whether they can study.

Many FE Colleges already have a useful volume of advanced work, even if they did not qualify for incorporation after the Education Reform Act of 1988. Others will quickly develop it in the climate of opportunity created by the incorporation of FE colleges after 1993 (HMSO, 1991b). New centres of economic growth at present without a local college of higher education will look for their own resource. Towns such as Milton Keynes, Swindon and Telford are likely to be the locations of significant development.

To the potential of the colleges of further education will be added that of the sixth form colleges when they, too, are incorporated and are able to develop their portfolios of work. They are well positioned to develop first years of degree courses through franchising arrangements, but have also the creative energy to find new and original ways forward for themselves.

Although new forms of competition are emerging so also are new forms of collaboration. Well-established institutions are looking for ways of pooling scarce resources in some highly specialized areas. In their search for students, universities, polytechnics and colleges of higher education are looking for students with BTEC diplomas, or mature students prepared for entry by means of special access courses and are developing special relationships with particular colleges to do so. More important, the power of major institutions to award franchises to colleges to teach whole courses or parts of them (typically the first year or the first two years of degree courses) is both speeding up the spread of higher education in other colleges and also bringing institutions together. In one case (Doncaster College) the Diploma of Higher Education has found onward routes for its students on more than 30 degree courses in 14 institutions.

But as time goes on structures may change, and colleges may find it helpful to form networks in which resources held in common are used over substantial areas and in many centres. This concept has already been applied in colleges of technical and further education in some states of Australia. In New South Wales, for example, the network has replaced the college as the primary planning coordinating and quality control unit of technical and further education. Teaching staff are appointed to the network as members of strong teams in each teaching area and may teach in any of its centres. Apart from one, Sydney Technical College, which with 50,000 student enrolments a year taught on 14 different sites *is* a complete network, colleges are part of larger organizations. But size can bring conformity. The polytechnics have perhaps been more successful than universities in fostering small staff teams with innovative ideas. But radical change is more difficult to achieve in larger programmes.

One of the weaknesses of contemporary higher education is its overspecialization. The arguments in favour of higher education which provides its students with a broader range of conceptual frameworks and of generic intellectual skills have been around for decades. Similar problems have been identified in the United States where it is more often the small college than the large university which has pioneered new approaches to the problem. Alverno College, Milwaukee, for example, which has been one of the leading institutions in developing curriculum and process so as to secure for students the simultaneous development of transferable skills and competence in areas of knowledge (Alverno College Faculty, 1989) is a small, Catholic, women-only college. The Alverno faculty are clear that innovations affecting a whole institution are only possible where the institution is small. So also in this country some of the institutes and colleges of higher education have found ways of balancing specialism with breadth and this suggests a likely distinctive role for such colleges in the future. It is here that the support of an imaginative validation system is most needed.

Among the changes in teaching style which are now extending in higher education are computer-aided learning and distance learning. The experience of the Open University, and of other more recently established opportunities for learning at a distance, is that learning can be lonely and needs tutorial support wherever it is attempted, especially to build up confidence. But the other major changes in teaching style have to do with awareness of the way differences of learning style and personality type affect the way that we learn. Here there is vast scope for innovation, and again American experience suggests it is in the smaller institution that experiments are best made and real and permanent changes introduced. They also have less prestige to protect and so can afford to adopt risk strategies rather than cautious conservative approaches – though note that several hundred colleges in the USA have closed in the last decade.

There is scope for further innovation outside the FE system. Small private institutions have always been one source of provision: a number now offer courses validated by the CNAA bringing their standing and quality within the mainstream of public recognition. There are seven privately maintained theological colleges currently recognized by the Council (CNAA, 1990) and other colleges offer courses in Art, Drama, Dance and in other subjects. It is in privately funded and run institutions that practitioners of alternative medicine are largely trained. Within the world of employment a number of companies and industries have founded their own colleges. There are a number of management centres in particular, but there have been other ventures too, such as the consortium of employers in the advertising, graphics and related industries who founded the School of Visual Communication in 1985 to develop creative designers of high calibre. The school claims to be based upon a 'very radical line of thinking' which enables its students to think freely and instinctively, while working on the actual problems of clients and to the deadlines and pressures of the business world.

It is consistent with the climate of the times that these institutions remain free standing and self-supporting rather than created and maintained by the nation as part of its provision. Equally, just as the University of Buckingham began life as a self-supporting university college and was absorbed into the general university system after some years of operation, in a system where any institution may compete for a share of the nation's funds other colleges may begin life independently and join the system subsequently.

The higher education system is going through a period of substantial change and is about to expand. Just as the other colleges of yesterday have become part of the mainstream of today so the other colleges of the 1990s will no doubt develop their own distinctive features before becoming part of the mainstream of the early twenty first century, leaving space for other colleges to emerge and innovate.

6

Further Education: Navigating the 1990s

John Gray

Where is FE?

For a week during August 1990 I found myself attempting to sell the virtues of partnership between potential clients in Czechoslovakia and FE colleges in the UK. The message to my Czech and Slovak hosts was that, to help them restructure a largely inefficient and over-centralized economy, they would need an education and training infrastructure like that of our FE system to provide for their 'requalification' needs. In particular I was arguing that to enable their economy to cope with decentralization there is a need to get information technology (IT) skills into the hands of a large number of middle managers and technicians and that, on the basis of ten years of experience in doing just that, our UK FE colleges could be ideal partners to help them. My hosts, naturally enough, asked 'What is an FE college?'

The question isn't a simple one! Defining an FE college is difficult, given the range of scale and activity that a college could be involved in:

> No two colleges are identical. Some are specialist institutions covering areas such as agriculture, building or art and design. Others have a wide range of programmes up to and including degree level work. One college will concentrate on vocational subjects; another will have a strong commitment to general education; while a third might emphasise its consultancy service to local industry. The ethos of a college will inevitably be influenced by the nature of the local community, industry and commerce. (Royal Society of Arts, 1989)

This enormous variety has left the service with something of an identity problem. Colleges are responsible for a large part of the post-compulsory education that isn't 'Higher Education' (and some that is, as Alan Parker recognizes in Chapter 10). Many of our potential clients seem to have a rather third-rate impression of our colleges and our services. A well-meaning but nonetheless irritating comment came my way from an industrial partner recently: 'there are Universities, and the Polytechnics, and then FE colleges are the next lot down . . .' For an uncharacteristically despondent moment I wondered whether he knew any more about us than my Czechoslovak friends . . .

Where are we going?

My protestations that in FE we aren't the next lot down in any sense but that we are in altogether a different business did little, I suspect, to change my correspondent's perception! Kenneth Baker realized there was a problem and tried to encourage us:

> Further Education is not just the bit in between school and higher education. It is not just the Cinderella of the education service, as I gather some people refer to it. As all of you realize, further education is of fundamental importance in its own right.　　　　　(DES, 1990)

He went on to talk of an FE initiative that should take place on the back of the Education Reform Act and in which action on the curriculum, qualifications, the image and marketing of FE should take place. Baker's speech seemed to go a long way to try, perhaps for the first time in recent history, to provide an official sense of purpose for our FE system. His comments about the importance of college-based vocational education and the need to develop core curriculum for FE met a receptive audience in FE:

> We want to equip young people with knowledge and skills so that they have greater chances. In the changing employment world they will need broadly-based qualifications. They will want to show their employers flexibility. They will need to be able to think and act independently. Otherwise, the next wave of technology will leave them stranded.
>
> 　　　　　　　　　　　　　　　　　　　　　　　　　(DES, 1990)

Identifying the importance of skills such as communication, numeracy, team working and leadership and by highlighting the critical importance of information technology skills, foreign language knowledge and flexibility across changing working and social contexts, Baker's speech encouraged us to think imaginatively about our future developments.

Vice President for Training and Development, Institute of Personnel Management, Ron Johnson, in evidence provided to a House of Lords Select Committee, stated that, compared with our continental counterparts:

> . . . we still have in this country an essential short term view and no consensus about the training and development of the work force.
>
> Over the last decade or two we have lurched from one programme to another and from one crisis to another.
>
> The lack of a concern for building up in individuals the background education and training they need, not just to do the immediate job but to continue their development, is a particular shortfall. (Johnson, 1990)

The Institute for Public Policy Research (IPPR) endorsed this viewpoint and explained the failure, especially in England and Wales, adequately to educate 16–19 year olds as a result of the entrenched but artificial divide between the 'academic study' represented by A level and the 'vocational' study represented by job-specific and relatively low level training. The IPPR study argued that Britain's divided education system reinforces the fatal characteristics of 'early selection and low participation' which make early entry to work more attractive to school leavers and cause undervaluing of continuing education:

> for too long, divisions between the Departments of Education and Employment have plagued policy making. Initiatives for sixteen to nineteen year olds have not been properly coordinated. The consequences being confusion and failure.   (IPPR, 1990)

and this at a time when

> education will be the foundation of material as well as intellectual progress. The challenge is to develop an education system adequate to the economic and social demands of the next century. The social requirement that the system help each individual realise their full potential is matched by the economic necessity that innovative capabilities be spread throughout the population.   (IPPR, 1990)

The report proposes the development of a new, unified system of education and training, leading to a single 'advanced diploma' or 'British Baccalaureat' which would encourage the formation of a 'late selection – high participation' education system apt for the twenty-first century. The proposal addresses head-on the education versus training issue:

> We suggest the creation of a unified Department of Education and Training for England to coordinate the provision both of education for the under 19s and training for adult workers. In order to support the proposals for a unified qualification structure, it would be necessary to amalgamate the functions of NCVQ and SEAC into a Joint Qualifications Board.   (IPPR, 1990)

Having spent a number of years teaching and examining GCE A level myself I can only endorse the concerns expressed about the over-narrow, over-specialist and predominantly old-fashioned nature of A level:

> A-levels do not serve the interest of those who take them. In some ways worse still, the notion of an academic élite on which they are based leaves 75 per cent of young people to make do with a mixture of vocational qualifications and courses, unrelated to the academic route to Higher Education.   (IPPR, 1990)

I moved into FE colleges from school teaching in 1975 and have never regretted the move. I valued the 'real world' atmosphere that the college environment provided then, and it is still the main reason why I enjoy my job! There are of course some negatives: how frustrating that the low status of technical education leads to so few really capable young people taking the BTEC route to higher education and work; and how frustrating that the British definitions of 'University' and 'Higher Education' are so limited and out of phase with definitions in continental Europe, thereby making it more difficult for FE to take advantage of European funding and initiatives; and, most frustrating of all, how, despite all the rhetoric, employer commitment to education and training is so limited and short term.

I had high hopes for the extension of the tertiary college concept as a way to get the best of FE and non-FE worlds. It seemed to offer so much by eliminating artificial divides and sidestepping the barriers of educational élitism. The relatively limited implementation of the tertiary concept to date is to be regretted. Within the FE system as it remains, I have no confidence that an obsession with the need to involve industrial partners at every stage of our activity, the relocation of power from the TA to the new regionally based Training and Enterprise Councils and the apparent reluctance of central government to invest in anything unless it's privatized in some way will allow us to create a post-compulsory system that suits the needs of the next century.

All change

What does the next century look like? What can we do to try and prepare our institutions for it? Change is no stranger to FE. The traumas of the 1980s, in which FE colleges were dragged by the then MSC into a harsh client-centred world and our system coped with the enormous stress of delivering YTS, are unforgettable! We even came to see that it was good to be slim and efficient as the Audit Commission demanded, though an FEU report reminded us that:

> By the time the Audit Commission reported, FE had already been forced into a radical rethink of its provision and methods ... FE managers had also already had to acclimatize to the kind of phraseology which indicated the directions in which central planners intended the service to go ... the Audit Commission report leant disproportionately on considerations of economy and efficiency, because no reliable measures of effectiveness were yet available. (FEU, 1989)

The rigour of the 1980s has had a huge impact on our colleges and, apparently, a considerable effect on our clients' perception of us. *After Lancaster House*, looking at industry's plans for training and its use of FE and Higher Education, notes that

> Industrial pressure means that training must be flexible, fast and relevant. This is because it costs money and has to meet ever-faster changes in operating practices. (DES/PICKUP, 1989)

but despite this:

Virtually all firms consider FHE institutions have greatly improved their approach to training for industry but the institutions may still have some way to go before they can match private provision.

(DES/PICKUP, 1989)

Responsiveness and proactiveness are now accepted as important objectives for the way we run our colleges. This is probably just as well since, according to Hayes:

The majority of organisations now operate in an environment character- ized by:
(i)   growing turbulence and complexity
(ii) growing competition
(iii) increasingly international markets
Change and a changing future has become, paradoxically, the one guaranteed condition.   (Hayes, 1988a)

A world view

It seems we can safely assume that change will accelerate throughout the remainder of the century and that the H.G. Wells quotation used in a conclusion to the IPPR study will become ever more appropriate:

Human history becomes more and more a race between education and catastrophe.   (IPPR, 1990)

The IPPR study argues that the continuing existence of healthy society and prosperous economy depends on the interrelationships between economic and social change, education and labour reform and participation and attain- ment in the learning system. I believe we can add to these factors those of acute political change and the largely hidden cost of global environmental degradation induced by the prevailing short-term view of the 'costs' of economic activity.

We don't often think of crises in world affairs as factors shaping our education and training structures. Yet the last major world economic crisis of the mid-1970s triggered the recession and unemployment that gave us YTS and all the other 'schemes' of the 1980s. The sharp drop in the birth rate accompanying that crisis in national confidence is now into the post- compulsory age groups having caused disruption all along the way; more so than in other European countries with parallel trends.

The Gulf crisis reawakened national awareness of our energy dependency. I find it perfectly possible to imagine that, over the next few years, we will begin to see new attitudes to transport systems and energy matters which will have significant effects on our patterns of work.

Fifteen years ago, in my first FE teaching job, I initiated courses for full-time students in environmental science and energy issues. It wasn't easy to get people to take those courses seriously. Now, in a period of intense interest in matters 'green', there seems to be a realization that the fabric of our whole industrial society (and therefore the education and training systems it requires) is about to come up for renegotiation.

As I discovered in my meetings in Bratislava (my wife's home town, capital city of Slovakia, where 1970s industrial development has left atmospheric pollution levels 12 times higher than the international limits), requests for environmental protection expertise and training support under Czechoslovakia's portion of the UK-funded Know How programme are high on their priority list. New emphasis on the technical skills required to guard our environment may bring about the increased status of technical education which I earlier argued was so lacking in Britain. In my own college (where we have a specialist involvement in building services engineering) staff have long been demoralized by continuing reductions in their National and Higher National student numbers as grant aid and industrial support have dried up. Now there's a feeling that, surely, their environmentally related skills will be in demand.

European matters are of considerable importance to our FE colleges. During recent years there has been an enormous increase in the level of student exchange between UK and EC institutions. As this develops further, the pressure for harmonization of qualifications and of the post-compulsory systems themselves will grow – this may well move our UK system a little closer to the IPPR goals outlined earlier. A number of entrepreneurial colleges now have staff whose whole job consists of seeking out 'Euro-money' and building up European networks with a view to maximizing their colleges' benefits from the creation of the Single European Market (SEM), at the end of 1992. The report of the Cambridgeshire 1992 Project focused on the implications of SEM for FE colleges in terms of institutional development, marketing and curriculum development, new developments in technology, mutual recognition and comparability of vocational qualifications, and staff development. It argued that

> Whilst many colleges are getting to grips with the opportunities, particularly in the field of awareness raising, exchanges and links, and marketing abroad, few have addressed the broader scale implications.
> (Cambridgeshire County Council, 1989)

Changes in Eastern Europe provide a graphic illustration of the need for adequate education and training as an enabler of commercial competence. In the over-centralized economies of Eastern Europe, where unemployment was formally banished and disguised by employing several people to do each 'real job', survival now depends on acquiring quickly the skills of a highly technological society. In Czechoslovakia's post-socialist environment the euphemism of 'requalification' refers to the process by which the state seeks to create new training structures that must, over a very short period, re-equip adults for productive work in a much more efficiency-conscious and decentralized economy. A cardinal objective of requalification is to mop up the massive unemployment the arrival of a free economy is set to create.

This, if allowed to persist, would risk the rise of extremists with 'solutions' and a return to totalitarianism. Perhaps this stark example of the need for education and training may be too far removed from the UK context of 2000 to be worthy of our attention . . . but perhaps not?

A course for the future

A newspaper summary of a Ruskin College Trade Union Research Unit report notes that, under Ford's Employee Development and Assistance Programme, if offered £200 a year to pay for education, training, or health and lifestyle pursuits:

> Education comes up as the clear priority for most of the staff – ranging from semi-skilled shopfloor workers to managers – who answered the questionnaire. While more than a third wanted help with both education and health/lifestyle pursuits, more than half of those who replied were interested purely in educational opportunities . . . Five out of six employees knew what they would choose first: more than three quarters opted for technical and business studies, languages or handicrafts. The four most popular individual subjects were computer skills, German, car maintenance and French.   (*Times Educational Supplement*, 1990)

It so happens that I often find myself semi-jokingly (that also means semi-seriously!) encouraging my daughter to fight against the gender conditioning of peer pressure and teacher expectations. I tell her her future could be a career based on Europe, her ability to speak languages and an ease with technology. I hope her secondary school experience won't leave her without a genuine grasp of the core skills that being a Euro-citizen demands. Perhaps you can see why the Ford workers' wishlist so appeals to me.

The flavour of the 1990s is 'Europe and IT'. The new National Association for Information Technology in Further Education was born out of a 1988 HMI-organized study tour of Germany and France in which a number of senior managers from the FE system participated. Our purpose was to investigate how successfully Germany and France were bringing the skills of IT into their post-compulsory curriculum. We came back convinced of the vital economic role IT skills would have throughout Europe as a necessary enabling factor of technological progress and economic health. Essential elements in an FE core skills profile, IT skills and a capacity for 'Euro-communication' must be there for young people in Britain to make the best of their own career potential and build a strong economy for the country. Presently none of these needs is adequately catered for within the FE system.

Learning routes

FE's lifeline to the future is its capacity to deliver quality learning support relevant to real-world training needs. Long after we've solved the short-term efficiency-oriented problems, and restructuring we'll still be grappling with the complexities of enabling learning.

Will it be the same kind of learning system? I hope not. I for one will feel no sense of loss for the chalk and talk driven class-oriented teaching situations that I met when I first came into FE – and which still exist in considerable numbers. When quality comes back centre-stage, we must have a whole range of new learning technologies to underpin the student-centred approach which we so often talk about. I hope that affordable multimedia and interactive video learning technology, coupled with very powerful desktop computers, can provide (probably for the first time) an adequate base for extension of individual learning in our colleges. The links between such flexible learning technology and many other aspects of the personalization of learning are visible, yet largely unexplored.

In the past such hopes for educational technology have foundered on cumbersome and/or unreliable equipment, inadequate funding or sheer lack of the personal touch! It could be these new technologies will fail also. However, because of the sheer sophistication of much of what is now being created, I believe it will have a substantial effect on what we do. The college of 1990 (with approximately 70 per cent of its total budget spent on paying academic staff to teach or support learning) could become a thing of the past. The college as a centre for audio-visual and interactive learning technology resources, accessible to clients who can drop in and out or access through telephone lines, is a technical possibility. Certainly, the college that finds ways of delivering package-based learning on a flexible drop-in basis really does find its way into new, extra, business. For that reason alone we can expect colleges to test the new technologies to the limit as they compete to steal a slice of each other's business.

Of course there are factors that will work to maintain the present character of colleges. In the Ford workers' survey

> The idea of relying on correspondence or other home-based learning only appealed to a small minority. One in six wanted the classes to be held in the workplace, but they were heavily outnumbered by those who wanted to study off-site – presumably in a college or some learning centre. (*Times Educational Supplement*, 1990)

The main activity of colleges: preparation of students for examinations (or other forms of assessment) leading to qualifications, is presently being absorbed into, and amended to meet, the competence-based approach favoured by the NCVQ. NCVQ philosophy depends on a unit-based structure of qualifications at a number of levels of competence. Modularization of the curriculum, accreditation of prior learning and work-based learning are aspects of the structure that emerge from the work of NCVQ's industry-led 'lead bodies'. Experimentation with these innovations is interesting and worthwhile – indeed my own college is directly involved in national projects examining some of these areas. However, past experience tells me to be a little cautious about the ever-present risk of throwing the baby out with the bathwater!

Predictably the IPPR study has a list of concerns about NCVQ. Although

the reorganization being undertaken by NCVQ is long overdue, and the concept of a training system based on national standards and local delivery has now achieved wide acceptance.   (IPPR, 1990)

the problems include:

NCVQ is not producing the types of qualifications that reflect the economic needs of the medium to long run.

NCVQ is specifying exceedingly narrow and low level task-based standards.

NCVQ requirements ask for little in the way of the general education that marks out French and West German training.

the provision for employer assessment of competences may lead to considerable problems, not least because many employers have neither the staff nor the incentive to provide for proper assessment. (IPPR, 1990)

Chris Hayes believes we're losing sight of the need to provide genuinely educated and flexible people who don't need to go through a brand new training course every time something changes in their business environment. He argues that we in Britain have failed to recognize that the most successful economies in the world produce generally-educated, rather than specifically-trained people.

In his report of a study carried out in Volkswagen he tells us that:

VW has expectations of creative and imaginative contributions from its staff and therefore sees competence as including technical proficiency, personal commitment and collaborative effectiveness.   (Hayes, 1988b)

In this considerably more ambitious interpretation of 'competence' than the NCVQ model, there is a need for the development within post-compulsory provision of 'overarching capabilities' including:

(a) thinking in network systems
(b) ability to act in complex business situations
(c) problem-solving ability
(d) flexibility and creativity
(e) independence and responsibility
(f) ability to communicate and cooperate.

Chris Hayes' Prospect Centre is now managing a study in three UK colleges (including Basford Hall College) in which the practical problems of addressing these complex objectives are being examined.

Who's steering?

So, the message is that the 1990s require the development of a higher status, balanced and non-divisive post-compulsory education provision which will attract more students, which will be recognized as of national importance and resourced accordingly. Without this there is little chance of breaking out of the cycle of 'early selection – low participation'.

Our chances óf achieving this don't look good. It's not easy for individual FE colleges to counteract the emphasis on short-term accountability which so often seems to steer our decisions. Since the Education Reform Act all our institutions have been gearing up for survival and/or maximization of short-term income in order to get themselves a more advantageous share of the training and education markets that exist. Corporate status will not change that. The initiative for delivery of vocational training has been passed to the Training and Enterprise Councils whilst, at the same time, the academic curriculum of A levels is the object of yet another round of national debate – this time centred on the value of AS levels as broadening of the schools' post-compulsory curriculum. This fragmentation of effort and the slavish adherence to an industrial sponsor model for providing the training the nation needs really ought to stop!

Arrowsmith (1990) states:

> the role of any educational institution should be defined in educational rather than financial terms. Indeed one of the conclusions of *Managing Colleges Efficiently* was that 'efficiency should not be considered in isolation but in conjunction with effectiveness'.

And yet that's what is happening – enormous emphasis on the efficiency component, with rather crude performance indicators beginning to drive the whole educational process. I don't want to minimize the importance of efficiency – I'm pushing as hard as anyone to achieve the efficiency targets. In doing so I'm taking a calculated gamble that we'll be able to come through the present phase of concentrating on efficiency aspects better equipped to capitalize on the demand for a more quality-oriented system that I expect to exist within 3 or 4 years:

> it is clear that the quality of the overall curriculum on offer is tied in with cost-effectiveness: not to be highly cost-effective means that either fewer clients are given opportunities ... or that existing learners experience a more restricted offer.   (FEU, 1986)

The performance indicators set by *Managing Colleges Efficiently* (DES, 1987a) include measurement of unit costs of courses. This involves student data, staff data, financial details of expenditure on materials. Any serious attempt to handle such complexity implies the existence of relatively sophisticated computer-driven management information systems. The influence of computer technology on the way colleges are run has made the possession of information handling skills almost a prerequisite for senior appointments in recent years. A colleague of mine in the National Association for IT in FE, Peter Shuker, often refers to the 'Young Turk' Vice Principals he meets all over the country. He warns his fellow college Principals how these newcomers are, through their familiarity with computer systems, insidiously taking over the actual operation of their colleges, often without their Principal's permission! This picture of the 1990s FE-yuppie reminds me of a now-ancient EDUCA article in which it was predicted that

> if you have ambitions to be a Principal, Vice Principal or Head of Department of the 1990s you will need to be IT super literate, as well as clear thinking, financially aware, superb public speaker, good at interpersonal skills . . .   (EDUCA, 1986)

All those needs are still there – plus at least one more, a good memory! Good enough, that is, to remember why you came into the job and to keep your mind permanently tuned to the real purpose of becoming business-like in the first place – providing quality education.

Enjoying the ride

A UK FE college is a turbulent place. When 70 per cent of all the money a college spends goes to pay its staff, lecturers and managers, it's pretty clear that the capacity of those staff to handle the turbulence is the main determinant of success.

For me, there's an excitement nowadays about being in a more genuinely independent situation than ever before. As the implementation of Local Management of Colleges (LMC) begins to take effect (and with the aid of increasingly powerful information systems) it's becoming possible for someone in my position to shape the college's strategy less constrained by external bureaucracy than previously. Paradoxically, the external steer of our main client, the Local Education Authority, is stronger than before, as it exercises the strategic planning role accorded to it by the 1988 Education Reform Act. That's fine by me – the LEA as a demanding client determined to improve post-compulsory provision is perfectly acceptable; the LEA as a sluggish limiting bureaucracy was quite another! And, as nearly monopoly providers of pre-16 education they must, despite government's stated intentions, continue to influence post-16 provision even though not controlling it through funding. Whilst there are certainly tensions in the post-ERA FE world, and may be more with full 'independence', life as a college manager is more rewarding. After years of seeing myself as 'being an educator' it comes as quite a surprise to find so much personal satisfaction from 'being in the education business'. So far, I'm enjoying the ride.

I wonder how many of my colleagues are enjoying their journey towards the next century? I can only *wonder* because my college, like most others, doesn't really have ways of *knowing*! Those colleagues who are stimulated by change, and who have personal and technical skills that enable them to exploit opportunities, may thrive in such a situation but, for many others, the ride seems to get rougher year on year as the certainties of the 1960s (when a large number of our older staff were recruited) disappear. Morale is pretty low in FE and the destruction of the FE career structure by agreements of recent years has had the effect of locking our staff into job immobility thus risking staleness and lack of initiative. Despite these negative pressures, a very high proportion of colleagues maintain an optimistic and professional approach to work and manage to cope with the undoubted stress their job now entails.

Lack of any genuine personnel management function and, particularly of an appraisal system linked to staff development and skills audit, leave my college presently unable to plan for 'getting the best' out of our staff. A clear priority for us in the future must be to create an environment in the college that encourages people, through self-evaluation and consequent professional development, to become able to influence their own role in the college and so increase the probability of their making a positive contribution to it. If we can delegate control of resources, give freedom to innovate within broad college policy frameworks and stimulate a sense of personal ownership and responsibility for managing change we stand the best possible chance of maintaining the FE college as the 'best value for money' provider for the country's urgent 1990s training and education needs. That is the challenge for the independent college corporations after 1992.

7

Policy for Vocational Education and Training: 'Have Tail to Wag – Where's the Dog?'

David Parkes and Gisela Shaw

What's wrong?

Using international comparisons – to facilitate diagnosis of and prescription for the ills of the vocational education and training systems of England and Wales – has been a growth industry since the Samuelson Commission reported the inadequacies of 1884. It seemed entirely appropriate that the Report *Competence and Competition* (NEDO/MSC, 1984) appeared as a centennial reminder. In that document, unfavourable comparison with competitor countries took in Japan, the USA and West Germany. Even though the relationship was tenuous between the research evidence and the recommendations for England and Wales, the latter provided an agenda for action by the then MSC in *After Competence and Competition* (Holland, 1985).

On a shorter time-scale, the diagnosis and prescription do not seem to have changed at all between the mid-1970s (Barnett, 1975) and the late 1980s (Finegold and Soskice, 1988). The problem is that the prognosis is dependent on the political and social context, i.e. the opportunity, the resources and the will to act (Parkes and Shaw, 1983).

Nevertheless, for the 1990s, Finegold and Soskice (amidst more general gloom) identify an opportunity window derived from demographic decline (and therefore resource redistribution) and lessening structural constraints. This does not add up to the major discontinuity which Parkes and Shaw identify as necessary to parallel the material collapse of Germany in 1945. They make the fundamental point that the modern West German system is *not* the product of centuries of tradition but of *post-war* necessity, the *discontinuity* of defeat and the need to establish clear structures for different parts of society to work together. They stress the need to construct infrastructures for cooperation, not conflict; and on planning before the event, not retrospectively rationalizing what has already happened. As in the case of France in the last 15 years – they make a case for the will to plan major change, not to argue for its impossibility.

The point for Britain is that, while removing privilege and 'conservatism' is necessary, it is *not sufficient*. Planning, infrastructure and investment are necessary to fill a century-old vacuum.

Finegold and Soskice find complements in Fonda and Hayes (1988) and Steedman (1988). A summary of these suggests:

1. A lack of participation in post-16 education and training, full- or part-time.
2. A lack of either State or private sector investment in training.
3. A lack of coherent training policies.
4. A lack of institutional means of implementing policies were they to exist.
5. A relationship between the type of low level manufacturing surviving and the lack of a perceived need for training.

Steedman compares mechanical and electrical crafts in France and Britain and points out that France trains three times the numbers (at craft and technician levels) and has made better progress in adjusting training programmes towards increased requirements for multi-skilled personnel. (West Germany trained four times the UK numbers in these areas.)

Fonda and Hayes argue for long-term strategies and for a 'champion' to develop political will for an appropriate infrastructure for the post-secondary education and training system. They also argue for a responsive system which is not only cost-effective and market orientated but also structured to bring into equilibrium long-term strategic planning with organizational capacities to handle uncertainties and discontinuities.

This is familiar stuff; diagnosis and prescription going back to Matthew Arnold and being picked up in 1990 by Claus Moser for the British Association for the Advancement of Science.

Recent British vocational education and training (VET) history does not offer many examples of planned intervention accompanied by investment except in the case of the New Training Initiative (NTI) where the investment was not high enough and, according to Deloitte, Haskins Sells (1987), not controlled and monitored. The rhetoric of the NCVQ is high profile but so far unproved in adding coherence to the systems and quality to the product. The exhortations for excellence have remained just that.

On the other hand, contemporary government policy for VET is not so far from our (competitor) European partners (van Hoof and van Wieringen, 1986):

1. Centralization and decentralization occurring simultaneously.
2. Privatization and soft-money schemes being a feature of all systems.
3. A market ideology, the predominance of employers' interests.
4. The location of decision-making in corporate institutions.

But, in England and Wales, these organizational factors impact on a particular cluster of weaknesses:

1. Low participation rates.
2. Complex overlapping provisions under the different regulations for the post-16.
3. Low employer contribution to training.
4. The relationships among the contributory parties (education institutes/ private sector/local authorities/examining and validating bodies) being complex enough to be virtually incomprehensible even to those in the network.

What do the statistics tell us?

A major project funded by the European Commission and by the European Institute of Education and Social Policy (EIESP) has profiled each of the post-16 (or 16–19) qualification systems in the Community (Gordon, 1989). For the English and Welsh there is exposed a lack of consistently collected and coherent information at different levels for the education and training systems. In the EIESP project it has been difficult to make sense of overlapping and inconsistent statistics available for the English scene and it has been comparatively invaluable to find how statistics are collected and used elsewhere.

This statistical confusion adds to the difficulties in 'getting hold' of the system and effecting change.

However, some very simple points emerge from the PETRA programme (of the European Community) 1990. PETRA statistics point out boldly that in the 12 Community countries:

(a) for *16 plus* participation in full-time education and training the UK just edges into the top four countries;
(b) for *17 plus* participation the UK drops to the middle four;
(c) for *18 plus* participation the UK drops well into the bottom four alongside Portugal and Greece (i.e. we are a country requiring aid with its development).

The major consideration for the English and Welsh systems is *volume of activity* (i.e. numbers of students and participation rates). At national level, BTEC and NCVQ were established (among other things) to raise the volume of activity and the number of qualified craftspersons and technicians. Despite these numbers doubling over the past ten years, we are left with the comparative figures above. Even 15 years ago, the Italian figures for students in 16–19 full-time education and training were in advance of the English figures. It would seem that British figures for VET are more comparable with Spain, Portugal and Greece than with West Germany, France and Italy.

It is useful to elaborate a specific example. We make a comparison directly with the Netherlands – a country with which we share a drive towards corporatism and decentralization (Gordon, 1989).

If we take the European Community vocational levels classification system (European Community, 1985), this defines attainment Level 3 vocational levels to include general and technical secondary education that leads on to higher education and also those vocational secondary and vocational education and training courses aiming either at labour market entry or higher education.

The qualifications to meet Level 3 by these criteria are:

Netherlands   *England and Wales*
VWO/HAVO   A level
MBO   BTEC National

The Netherlands 16–19 population in 1986 was 988.3 thousand.
The UK 16–19 population in 1986 was 3,576.5 thousand.
The UK 16–19 population was *3.6 times higher.*

The comparison of Netherlands with the UK for 1986 for Level 3 qualifiers was:

UK   242.7 thousand
Netherlands   121   thousand

In the UK there were only twice as many qualifiers for a population 3.6 times bigger.

The breakdown between general/technical education and VET is interesting. The UK figure of 242.7 thousand divides into: 198 thousand A level, 44 thousand BTEC. The Netherlands figure of 121 thousand divides into: 71.6 thousand VWO/HMVO, 49.7 thousand MBO; Apparently a much stronger VET tradition.

Incidentally, it is impossible to compare Level 2 statistics (skilled worker) since the British largely count certificates and not people.

What kind of system do we have compared with the others?

These critical analyses are always subject to the comment that they fit different cultural and structural conditions. But, as above, too much excuse can be made for inaction. We do not, actually, want to be faced with the 'discontinuity' posited by Parkes and Shaw (1983) before taking action.

In dividing up the world, perhaps mischievously, between the English and French (decentralized and centralized), we would offer three conceptual frames which provide a positioning in the broader world context. Figure 7.1 (p. 76) offers the major conflicting elements in most education systems.

Although the fiercest debate is between B and C at a glance one can place centralized systems such as the French predominantly within category A and the UK and perhaps the Netherlands predominantly in C. It is more difficult and more complex to place the USA (apparently highly decentralized) and

Figure 7.1   Major conflicting elements in educational systems.

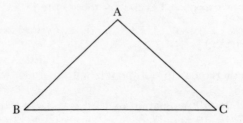

Public service led –
egalitarian in intention and redistributive –
key term : 'bureaucratic' –
'administration' dominated

A

B   C

Development of the
individual in the community –
key term: 'pedagogic' –
'professional' dominated

Industry and enterprise led –
key term: 'marketing' –
'management' dominated

West Germany just because they are federal countries and the mix of A, B and C is more evenly distributed than might seem the case at first glance.

Further examination also makes it more difficult to place the UK which, while ideologically leaning towards a 'parody' of USA decentralization, is, in fact, much more closely identifiable with a medium-size centralized European state.

Table 7.1 is interesting as it pushes the relations among central, intermediate bodies and institutions towards the bottom right-hand corner of the diagram and illustrates the English preference for concentrating on location of decision-making (i.e. process) rather than the generation of qualified young people (i.e. output).

However, there is an important implication other than the enterprising autonomy of institutions and governing bodies. The model indicates a fluid set of relations in which intraorganizational relations become a critical feature. In other words, managers no longer simply 'manage' their institutions, they have to manage the boundaries among themselves and the competition/cooperation that exists with other bodies both in the public and private sectors. Consequently, the boundaries between State and region; the boundaries between public and private; the boundaries between public education and commercial activity are wholly opened up.

This model, rhetorically at least, in the case of the Netherlands and the UK, gives management a 'pole position' over *'professional'* values. This is a most 'uncontinental' state of affairs, since German and French examples offer the ideal of a skilled professional working within an *administered* system.

Another positioning point is rather less a model than a cluster of forces

Table 7.1 Organization of educational systems

Site of control	Way of coordination	
	By rules	*By exchange*
Concentrated	1. Central control by formal authority	2. Central coordination by resource-manipulation
Dispersed	3. Voluntary cooperation	4. Adjustment by market mechanism

Source: van Hoof and van Wieringen (1986).

operating simultaneously. What is clear in both the Netherlands and the UK systems is an uneasy coming together of *centralization* and *decentralization* (or deregulation) with *privatization* and the application of soft-money *resource manipulation*. These factors are often in disharmony and not easily understood. The Education Reform Act (1988) presents an interesting case of the factors at work in all three categories being presented together in a major piece of legislation.

All the factors lead to the rejigging of authority and power exemplified in corporate institutions with a high degree of autonomy, powerful governing bodies and bottom-line budgets.

The difficulty, particularly in the case of the UK, is that responsiveness to employers' needs from public sector organizations is seen through the metaphor of *'private enterprise'*. Institutions are being asked to be competitive not only with the outside world, but with each other. A metaphor is fine, but, as with all metaphors, stretched too far it becomes meaningless.

John Bevan (1988) suggests that a corporate college may be a freestanding legal entity – but it is not in any necessary way 'free'. Political control goes with the bestowment of public money. Corporate institutions are not free from constraints; they are to do with the location of the power to impose constraints. The college becoming a separate legal entity is not the same thing as being independent or autonomous. In simple practical terms, autonomy within the law comes with financial independence from a dominant funding body, whether public (central or local government) or private (e.g. a holding company). None of our institutions is free in that sense (although they may, on the other hand, be cut adrift).

Despite the fact that the rhetoric of 'corporatism' existed earlier and, in some ways, exists more fully in the Netherlands than in the UK corporate institutions exist in a context of national far-reaching education and training reforms which have a number of complementary features, such as:

(a) long-term objectives;
(b) programmed time and mechanisms for curriculum development among representatives of education, employers and employees;

(c) decisions made on the basis of market and occupational research;
(d) time-scales and mechanisms of planning and implementation for change in vocational training on a longer time-scale in Britain;
(e) decisions made on the basis of large-scale research and information procurement initiatives funded by the Netherlands government;
(f) a simpler and more logical system of curriculum development;
(g) overall, long-term strategic planning for vocational education and training based on funded research and data.

How might we get to change things?

All this is to make the point that the relocation of power and authority is not a resolution, nationally, of the failure to address systemic issues. To name but two:

(a) an integrated, consensus-based strategy and operational mechanisms for delivery;
(b) investment.

The point on investment is hammered home by every commentator since Matthew Arnold. The government accepts the criticism. However ... it appears to await the discontinuity.

But even if investment were to increase significantly with new government policies, issues of regional structures and integrating mechanisms to bring together national, regional and local strategies would need to be addressed. In 'historic' England and Wales, the examining and validating bodies have retrospectively held together the otherwise inchoate mess. There is a tendency in Britain for central bodies to be sentinels around which the system dances in order to organize itself. In English vocational education and training there is no equivalent to the Bundesinstitut für Berufsbildung (BIBB), which is the integrating organization that helps determine the curriculum content for all training programmes in the 'German Dual System'. Before the training starts, BIBB brings together the Länder and the employers (and indeed the unions) to corporate agreement in a coherent system. That system is largely funded by investment from employers although with considerable subsidy from the State. What equivalent in English institutions exists to the Centre d'Etudes et de Recherches sur les Qualifications (CEREQ) which in France simultaneously and systematically advises the Departments of Employment and Education on the relationships between occupational sector changes and required training programmes?

Given a concept of strategic planning one has to look at the possibilities of intervention at the different levels in the system and perhaps actually have a plan. In Britain, NAFE planning is a helpful and positive development, but how far is it from the national plans produced from the French 'Commissariat au Plan' or the German 'Bund-Länder Kommission' which bring together the regional and national interests in a common forum? Decision-making exists alongside the curriculum. In Germany, there is a linear development to craft and technician levels where one stage follows another in a very clearly defined way; the French have an internal updating system through *formation permanente* where investment (again from industry) is of an updating kind. The British have drifted in this direction but nevertheless ten times the number of French workers had their qualifications updated between 1975 and 1985 than in equivalent English industry.

The issue, then, is how to establish conditions where the diagnosis, prescription and prognosis tendered by commentators and even accepted by 'powerful champions' in government can be put into effect. There is a wealth of literature on managing change, whether macro or micro. Lauglo (1977) argued that contrasting organizational forms might be required for macro and micro reforms in education. A high degree of bureaucracy makes structural reform possible while non-bureaucratic forms are needed for curriculum innovation and the teacher learning process itself.

Cerych and Sabatier (1986) conclude that it is only possible to achieve far-ranging change in a narrow and targeted area and only where there is an equilibrium between radical change and traditional forces. Examples are the establishment of the Council for National Academic Awards (CNAA) and the Open University in Britain, when new approaches were bulwarked by conservative academic values. What we need, however, is something more cataclysmic.

The nearest we have to a major structural overview came in 1981 from a *New Training Initiative: An Agenda for Action* (MSC, 1981a). NTI established three areas for action to restructure the UK training scene. *Training for Jobs* (DE, 1984) was also a major instrument for centrism and vocationalism outside the traditional pattern (an earlier response to Finegold and Soskice's (1988) later requirement for a strengthened central bureaucracy). The NTI's three-prong attack on youth training, initial skills and adult training all now look decidedly blunted. Neither will nor resource were sufficient.

Managing change in the 1990s has to take on board the implications of the Education Reform Act (1988), and the Further and Higher Education Acts (1992), particularly, in this case, on FE. Sometimes, one feels that the English are dazzled by their apparent understanding of the decentralized systems of North America without taking on board the cultural, historic and structural dissonances which they are so eager to highlight in their European neighbours.

As we have seen, the Acts are concerned with the transfer of authority and power and aspire to an FE service which is more responsive, more relevant and of higher quality. But excellence requires a combination of both quality and *quantity*. The latter remains an aspiration only. The Acts are *not* a legislative framework like that of Germany which regulates at national, regional and institutional levels and relates the role of colleges, employers and chambers of industry and commerce to a common vocational curriculum which has common political support.

The new TECs have some metaphorical relationship with German or indeed French chambers of industry and commerce. NCVQ is an attempt to provide overall qualification coherence for an internal updating within industry of competences and qualifications.

The employer-dominated TECs have put in the decision-making firing-line that category of British society (representing British industry) which (comparatively) has most significantly failed over the last 100 years to deliver the goods. It marginalizes those categories of English society where comparative excellence has been perceived by our foreign competitors. Rather than an increased investment the employers themselves are complaining about the government's removal of vital resources from an existing low base. The TECs are a wonderful example of government ideology and policy through the 1980s, i.e. within a faith in the *market* to launch a series of initiatives, all untested and untried; then to argue that there is little point in criticizing them since they *are* as yet untested and we must have faith that they will work in the future. Whether it is TECs or NCVQ or 'opting out', there is no relationship between national faith and the actual practical establishment of national/regional infrastructures with a resourcing base. It is sending an army into battle with neither arms nor battle plan, but strengthened with tracts.

In different systems one needs to investigate the regulatory framework which places institutions in a context and which gives or fails to give 'statutory' clout. The TECs have been mentioned as an interesting analogue with West German chambers of industry and commerce. At this point we might contemplate changes in Eastern and Central Europe – where discontinuity is enabling wholesale revision of occupational sectors and training structures supported by Community aid and bilateral support from individual Community countries. The old East Germany is a telling example where the West German structures are simply replacing what is generally there. The Eastern bloc countries, particularly East Germany, had a German tradition with significant Soviet influence, i.e. central planning without flexibility where employers could not take initiatives but were simply told what to do.

In the old East German territory, the Chambers are to be set up anew as the education and training systems are revamped from top to bottom. As in West Germany, the employers are in the saddle, their role is legislated and firms are motivated to take on trainees. The infrastructure is *not* central but regional and local within a national framework. Regionally, chambers are being set up with help from Bonn.

Of course there are enormous human and resource problems but the Germans are putting structures into place with clear ideas of what they want, how to make it work and to a clear timetable.

It is an example of starting from a perilous position and with a clear discontinuity and with a dramatic shift from an ideology which previously blocked off radical action.

In Germany there is being assembled a dog with a tail; in the UK the TECs are as yet just a tail without even a dog to wag. Ideology is in the way of finding the dog to join the tail to.

The authors have been involved with two major change strategies for the UK, both funded by the Training Agency: one in the UK, one from Paris, i.e. from outside, looking in:

1. *The Responsive College Programme*, funded to circa £2.5 million.
2. *Strategies for VET in Europe.*

Both have been designed to centre on the development of change either in specific localities or in specific occupational sectors. In short, the emphasis post-ERA has had to be on bottom-up (micro) change at the expense of top-down (bureaucratic). One is forced to models for change which accept English diffuseness and use robust approaches which deploy practitioners as the fulcrum around which the investigations are carried through and recommendations made. Those recommendations either on marketing management information systems or curriculum content are important enough and they are consistent with eventual systemic change. But the latter cannot occur without the realization of:

(a) the inadequacy of metaphors;
(b) the need for investment;
(c) the need for strategic planning;
(d) the need for integrating mechanisms;
(e) the necessity for stability and systemic development.

Investment, strategic planning and integrating mechanisms require long-term perspectives and a measure of stability, not endless wheezes and certainly not attitudes – occasionally exemplified in government – of an amateurish, uninformed, careless and nonchalant kind. Conservative, Labour and Liberal Democratic parties now exhibit a certain will: but we now need a phase when good ideas are given sustained sustenance, not new ones given fleeting substance.

8

Adult Education and European Communities

Leni Oglesby

Introduction: The European scene

The current political, social and economic scene in Europe includes a number of significant features which materially affect the adult education world. The 1970s were characterized by economic upheavals; the 1980s by a continuing general rise in unemployment levels, with all the consequent disturbance which that had for many of the adult population, their families and their communities; and the 1990s bid fair to have to cope with, amongst others, the following major issues:

1. East–West detente and the implications of perestroika and glasnost. Unprecedented change has taken place in Eastern Europe which has astonished many simply by the speed with which it has occurred. The new political talk now refers not only to an expanded Common Market but to 'a common European home'. However, almost inevitably there has been some degree of pendulum swing and fears that such speed betokened instability, given the desire for western type democratic governing and the lack of a infrastructure to support such systems.
2. Changing welfare policies in European countries and the implications for education in social and personal terms, and particularly the care and education of the socially disadvantaged and those with special needs. There is an expected large growth in the pensioner population which will inevitably have repercussions for tax and welfare policies.
3. Internationalism and competition throughout the whole of Europe, with the introduction of the EC single market in 1992. The removal of trade restrictions and the opportunities that will create for a mobile labour force will ripple increasingly through the member countries of the EC throughout the 1990s. That in turn will have major implications for those European countries outside the EC.
4. The changing regulations on EC nationality and the implications these will have for ethnic and political groups in minority positions in the countries in which they are living.

5. Major changes in educational policies in many countries, with predominant emphasis on education for industrial and commercial ends. This has meant financial difficulties for much of adult education provision in some countries.
6. The changes in demographic patterns. With the exception of Eire, the proportion of those under the age of 25 years has declined in all countries in Western Europe. After 1994 numbers start to rise again but at a slow rate. In EC countries the number of over-65s is expected to climb from 43 million in 1985 to 51 million in the year 2000, and will remain a high proportion of the population for some time thereafter (de Jouvenel, 1988).
7. Industrial restructuring. There have been marked shifts in occupational growth and decline, with an increasing rate of job obsolescence in Eastern Europe, and a growth of part-time work in western Europe. Unemployment is expected to rise very significantly within Europe and is unlikely to fall until the year 2000 at the earliest. There is a continued growth of female employment but at differing rates within the countries.
8. New technology, and the implications this has for educational systems and support services.
9. Ecological awareness and its subsequent effects on social and industrial initiatives, especially in the energy field.

To cope with these factors and the challenges they present, a majority of governments are placing emphasis on matching their education systems to their economic, industrial, and commercial systems at all levels. The emphasis on industrial values has permeated the education world with its talk of rationalization; improving efficiency and effectiveness; optimizing financial expenditure and value for money; business plans, devolution of costs, performance indicators, and quality products. One common trend has been the direction of resources to, or legislation on, particular types of education in order to 'safeguard' them, quite often through some type of national curriculum. Western European systems are developing increasingly along similar lines, and the problems are also proving similar, despite the cultural differences.

The current debate centres on two roles for education. In one, education is seen as a delivery system based on government policy which operates on a bureaucratic and managerial model. Decisions about what is to be taught is a management function, and the teacher/tutor is a technician whose role is to deliver it. The second sees education as a participatory and collaborative operation in which responsibility is shared among all those involved. Teaching is a profession with professional responsibilities and teachers have a central role. Systems for teacher education mirror this debate with reviews of the aims, role, certification and quality control of the profession. The UK is moving from a decentralized towards a centralized system in terms of the curricula and standards but towards community autonomy in respect of the governance of schools and colleges. Italy, Spain and France appear to be moving from centralism to regionalism in terms of their overall direction and control systems.

Overall, education policies in Western Europe appear to be moving towards a model whereby the respective governments define the global framework and the implementation/interpretation is delegated to the local or regional level. This regional basis for operation reflects the preferred mode of the EC and its programmes.

The role of adult education in Europe

Adult education's primary roles in this context are to help people to understand:

(a) the new economic order and the causes of this change;
(b) its consequences and related implications;
(c) changes in their political worlds and social and personal circumstances.

The questions such challenges pose to adult education include:

(a) what are the major issues facing the field of adult education in Europe;
(b) what can the adult education field do to aid development in Europe;
(c) what are the implications of those changes for the role and staff development needs of adult educators.

Adult education programmes will need to promote:

(a) discussion and reflection of people's responses to the inter-cultural dialogue in Europe;
(b) the attempts to deal with the divergent problems often found in the northern and southern regions of Europe;
(c) the changing relationship between east and west;
(d) freedom of movement and of the labour market;
(e) people's rights within the European Community and their regional and local communities.

In terms of people's working lives, changing forms of production in Europe mean new working and living conditions. However, these will be materially affected by the impact of demographic trends which indicate, throughout most European countries, that there will be a shortage of appropriately skilled young labour, and in particular, a call for more women to return to or be retained in the labour force. In some countries the start of the 1990s heralds either the return or the introduction of a economic recession.

In 1992 members of the EC will experience the effects of the introduction of the Single Market. The non-EC countries in Western Europe are reviewing their trade practices in the light of the expected impact of this. The lowering of barriers between east and west Europe also has implications not just for the internal economic, industrial and commercial structure of those countries but also for the position of southern European countries. They now see their position as being usurped in economic and development terms and a shift of resources being moved from them in the rush to bolster central and Eastern Europe. Anxiety is increasingly being expressed by the southern countries and the non-EC nations that they will be, to differing degrees, economically or politically marginalized by a central core of 'power' nations in Europe.

The 1990s: Priorities, issues and tensions

Analysis of documentation shows very clearly where the EC put its priorities for the education of adults for the period up to 1992:

> In looking forward to 1992... education and training must play an increasingly pivotal role in the overall development strategy of the Community in the years ahead... Without investment in the present and future workforce, Europe's capacity to innovate, compete, and to create wealth and prosperity... will be severely impaired. This emphasis on human resources provides an essential bridge between economic and social policies and is also a factor in promoting the free movement and exchange of ideas in addition to the four freedoms (goods, services, capital and persons) provided for in the Treaty of Rome.   (EC, 1989a)

Despite the references to education as well as training, the EC is proscribed by the terms of the Treaty of Rome from having a direct role in the education policies of member states. Although the distinction between education and training is now becoming increasingly blurred in its resolutions and programmes, it has concentrated primarily on training objectives and provision. Continuing vocational training was deemed to have four main functions:

1. 'Ensuring... adaptation to the changing nature and content of occupations and... the improvement of skills and qualifications...'
2. 'Promoting social conditions to enable large numbers of workers to overcome a lack of prospects for improving their qualifications and improve their situations.'
3. 'Forestalling any negative consequences of completion of the internal market and to overcome the difficulties in sectors or undertakings undergoing economic or technological restructuring.'
4. 'Integrating the unemployed...'   (EC, 1990)

More general adult education did not figure in EC policies except perhaps as an adjunct to basic education literacy work or within a small programme concentrating on adult residential schools. Development of vocational training policies was seen as the means by which the economic entity of the EC could be achieved through the mobility of a European labour force. To this end various programmes were put forward in terms of information technology; literacy and basic education; vocational preparation; women entrants to the labour market; and retraining for specific groups of adults unemployed in regions where there had been a collapse of a massive industry, e.g. steel and iron in the UK.

On the other side of the continent, Jindra Kulich (1985) identified, for the Eastern European countries, a similar dichotomy between cultural programmes on the one hand and vocational–technical upgrading adult education training programmes on the other.

These issues were still in place at the start of the 1990s. There is continuing tension between the cultural education work promulgated by many countries in both east and west Europe based on their socio-cultural liberal education traditions, e.g. sponsored by the Council of Europe and the European Cultural Foundation, and the vocational education emphasis being stressed and directed in financial input terms by governments and supranational bodies such as the EC.

The notable changes in emphasis which can be seen from the beginning of the 1990s were engendered by the features of the European scene outlined at the start of this chapter. In essence these were:

1. The political upheavals in Europe. The re-joining of West and East Germany made nonsense of programmes designed for technically sophisticated economies but now eligible to be applied to the eastern part of Germany.
2. The demographic patterns and the need to focus programmes on a potential labour force which would include an increasing proportion of:
    (a) Women. Programmes essentially designed to fit a workforce traditionally geared towards the working patterns and habits of men were undermined because of cultural expectations and domestic demands of women.
    (b) Immigrant and ethnic minority groups. For these groups literacy, second language teaching, and in some cases, basic education were required before any strictly vocational training could begin.
3. Industrial change. The need to improve rates of access and participation in education and training programmes required general education for groups of people who had mainly undertaken unskilled work and were the first to find themselves redundant.

The EC Task Force proposed a new Community action programme for the development of continuing vocational training (FORCE) for 1991–92:

> aimed at . . . improving access to continuing vocational training for all workers . . . ensuring access for the least skilled workers and guaranteeing equal treatment as regards access . . . It is so devised as to involve all the parties concerned (firms, training bodies, the two sides of industry and public authorities) . . . The programme will also be able to promote the spread of innovatory agreements and good practices.
>
> (EC, 1990)

The objectives of the FORCE programme are fivefold:

1. Develop partnerships designed to encourage greater awareness of the benefits accruing from investment in continuing vocational training.
2. Encourage dissemination of good practice.

3. Encourage innovations in the management of training, methodology, and equipment.
4. Support transnational and transfrontier training projects and the exchange of information and experience.
5. Help training mechanisms become more effective.

The trend began to emerge of a 'partnership' between industrial managers and the workforce in progressing labour market training policies, and the movement towards 'regionalism' accelerated. The 'top-down' imposed model of continuing vocational training programmes centred on industrial or occupational bases appears not to have promoted the degree of productivity required, and the emphasis is now on 'partnership' between employer and employee, institutions and levels of education, as being the preferred mode of operation, and the fostering of a network of partnerships to pool resources and expertise. Both the EUROTECNET (new technologies) and the FORCE programme stress the new partnership:

> where new forms of cooperation will be needed to combine the resources of the public and private sectors and link enterprises (large and small firms alike) education, research bodies and local communities in a collective investment in education and training.

and stress 'regionalism', with its:

> responsiveness of education and training to regional economic development measures, especially in areas of long-term unemployment, inner city decline and rural deprivation. (EC, 1990)

The implied results for the education and training field are cited as:

- Human resource development.
- Expansion in the volume of education and training.
- Continuity, with initial training preparing for and leading towards adult and further education.
- An emphasis in training on coping skills and adaptability.

Among those areas that are singled out for treatment are: basic education and initial training; the new technologies; and the promotion of equal opportunities covering women, immigrant and refugee basic education and the disabled.

Some of these adult education issues are echoed in east European countries where currently the main concerns include:

- The role of adult education in political education in helping to reformulate new forms of government akin to the western systems, and building a new social order.
- Building new economic growth through the training and retraining of workers.
- The level of functional illiteracy.
- Approaches that might help the plight of the currently unemployed, and

those for whom the prospect looms large. The western development of guidance and counselling for adults is coming more to the fore in the east as the automatic expectation of a job is being rapidly undermined.

● Work connected to the immigrant and ethnic minority populations.

In the light of the pressures arising from the political changes in the east the EC urgently amended its overall programmes in order to facilitate member state co-operation with a number of Eastern European countries under different programme headings. The priorities for action for joint training are in the fields of financial sectors, agriculture, environment, retail trade, heavy industry, telecommunications, and new information technologies.

One of the top priorities for action by the EC is the need to promote access to and participation in continuing education and training, through such means as European-wide open learning systems, information exchange on good practice, expansion of higher education, and opportunities for acquiring new types of qualifications. Particular arenas for action are equality of employment issues, in terms of attracting non-traditional groups, particularly women and members of ethnic minority groups, into higher level skills and technically orientated training; and language skills together with a concomitant broader set of skills and experiences necessary for promoting intercultural living and communication.

These issues are also supported by educators within the European adult education field (Oglesby, 1989) who determined the grassroots priorities for the early 1990s as:

1. Social and ethical concerns of culture, identity and language.
2. Occupational matters centring on the labour market, productivity and development of competence; education for agricultural and rural regions; trade union education; marginalized people within societies and the educational opportunities offered to them; vocational and educational guidance and counselling.
3. Mobility factors, and in particular European recognition and standardization of training programmes.
4. Access issues, linked to adult basic education, literacy, and information technology.
5. Health and environment issues facing not only Europe but the world, and the relationship of both of these to the industrial world.

A survey of the ERASMUS programme identified a number of needs for future programmes amongst which featured the need to foster a sense of cultural identity as Europeans; and the promotion of genuine mobility in Europe. Moves towards mobility have tended to reflect crises in occupational shortages rather than a basic tenet of policy.

Towards the year 2000

The issues that appear to be emerging in the approach to the year 2000 include both long-standing concerns, perhaps with a differing emphasis, and new ones reflecting the socio-economic and political scene as it appears to be developing. Some of the themes and tensions which are likely to be current in the 1990s and the year 2000 are discussed below.

Education versus training

The rigidity of the division between training, which is part of the EC's brief, and education, jealously guarded as the prerogative of member states, is now beginning to bend. The formalities of the division are being side-stepped by the practicalities required to bring about effective results. The emphasis on objectives that were geared only to the needs of industrial training ignored, at great cost to the policy objectives of the EC as well as its potential labour force, the need to improve education/industry links. The constant theme of feedback to Commission offices from adult education agencies was the need to knit the two approaches more. Attempts to increase access to vocational education were being constantly undermined by lack of a grounding of general education on which to build specific training needs.

It is proposed to group the Community's vocational training programmes into three main fields of activity: initial training; higher education; and continuing training, on the grounds of rationalization and a clearer framework in which to manage future initiatives. This tripartite division is likely to set the framework for the remainder of the century, and all three branches will be informed by concern for the value and importance of general education as a preparatory base for those returning and entering the labour market in later life; and general education as part of vocational education given the economic, social and political aims of the common market.

Instrumental versus developmental aims

The new thrust of EC policy seems to show a further marked shift from the strictly instrumental approach. Discussions in 1991 appear to indicate the preparation of proposals to emphasize the concept of citizenship, and education for the 'whole life' as opposed to the work side only. Proposals for programmes are beginning to echo the theme of 'éducation permanente' for citizens, given that the social dialogue at the beginning of the 1990s is not focusing solely on productivity but also on workers' 'well-being' within the community.

The purpose of this is to go some way towards meeting the perceived need for raising the level of readiness within adult education to cope more effectively with questions concerning a new Europe, on politics, economy, labour market, culture and society.

Liberal/cultural versus vocational

There is a tension between the cultural education work promulgated by many countries in Europe because of their socio-cultural liberal education traditions and the vocational emphasis being stressed and directed, in financial input terms, by supra-national bodies such as the EC.

Europe is perceived to be failing in its attempts to remedy serious skill shortages even in a time of increasing unemployment. The occupational shortages evident are still the familiar ones of scientists, engineers, technologists, and technicians. 'There is little evidence that Community education and training systems are responding adequately to the accelerating pace of technological change, or that industry was taking appropriate action to update the skills of the existing workforce . . .' (Commission of the EC, 1990).

The East has a marked tradition of viewing adult education as an integral tool of planned social as well as economic change, and it seems clear that the EC has noted this. East Europeans are very concerned with the role of adult education in political education, building a new social order, and building new economic growth through the training and retraining of workers. The greatest specific concerns appear to be the level of functional illiteracy, increasing unemployment, and raising public awareness or the need for upgrading the workforce.

An appreciation of the dangers of increased polarization of the labour force between the increasingly highly qualified and the unqualified is evident in both east and west. The needs of those without basic qualifications will have to be answered if there is to be a chance of enabling their economic and social progress and participation in the European labour market. The emphasis has to be on a human resources strategy which incorporates both bands of personnel (Lauglo and Lillis, 1988).

Partnership

The partnership and 'enhanced co-operation' angle is being strongly stressed as a major way forward in dealing with the difficulties of the complex social and economic union of the EC and its vocational training needs. This partnership angle is also being extended to its own work in that the EC proposes to co-operate with the Council of Europe which covers more regions of Europe than the EC does, and especially in the field of distance learning. Distance learning is seen as a crucial development tool for training in Europe in the 1990s, not least because it offers the possibility of ensuring a European dimension to training programmes, counterbalancing the diversity of training systems, and promoting partnership ventures between employers and employees.

Regionalism and Supra-nationalism

The concept of regionalism is one that figures strongly in programmes dealing with the labour market: education for a community, within a community and organized by a community. However, where the concept of regionalism is used as an operating mode it has both positive and negative aspects. There are very positive cultural and economic benefits attached to the region being the geographical focus and basis for the organization of education and training systems and provision. However, it is also envisaged that urban regions with a strong industrial or commercial focus will be *primus inter pares* and draw to themselves further resources, while those regions that are remote from the major urban centres will become more marginalized (Piehl, 1989).

Supra-nationalism has given rise to concerns, for example, about national sovereignty, cultures, minority languages, whether the distinction between the EEC and EFTA is sustainable, and whether such western European concerns are too parochial and we should be looking towards the 'common European home'. Apart from its links with eastern European countries, e.g. the TEMPUS programme, the EC is proposing to co-operate with EFTA countries on the ERASMUS and COMETT higher education and enterprise programmes.

The debate tends to centre round the question and viability of the larger grouping as opposed to more manageable geographical units which individuals can more easily relate to. The issue is one of centralization versus decentralization.

Equality

In this arena the issues are clustered around political, social and civic education, and informed by the issues of equity and access:

- Education for women and their position within society; namely, the new initiative, NOW, on vocational training and employment opportunities for women.
- Special needs issues; HORIZON is a programme for promoting the social and professional integration of the handicapped and other disadvantaged persons.
- Anti-racist programmes; and education initiatives for migrant workers. New trends in the labour market can bring, as a consequence, marginalization of migrant groups (Gelpi, 1990).
- The education of older people.

Underlying all these is a strong concern over the respective participation rates of these groups in education and training. Programmes will be encouraged to target those groups who have traditionally not participated in or had very low participation rates in post-compulsory education. It is envisaged that there will be EC funding support for innovatory programmes which will promote such developments.

It is in this arena that educational and vocational guidance and counselling systems will be promoted. Without these, adults throughout Europe will find themselves ill-equipped to make informed choices about their work, their leisure, and most importantly, the quality of their lives in a new Europe

(Watts *et al.*, 1986; Rivis, 1990). The PETRA programme, whose objectives include preparation for working life, has been strengthened to undertake this task (EC, 1990).

Staff development

There have been many documents and reports that have focused on the implications of the Single Market: the difficulties inherent in personnel planning and human resource development; the training programmes required to answer urgent needs; and the support systems to go with those including access programmes, family care arrangements, etc. However, in comparison, there have been far fewer papers on support systems and staff development for the educators or trainers coping with educational and training needs of the young and mature adults. Where it is included in EC programmes of work it tends to be as a 'tail-end charlie' in a list of objectives.

The reasons for this have been indicated by Legge (1985) and Kulich (1985) for countries in Western and Eastern Europe respectively. They cite:

- The tensions between liberal education and work-related vocational education provision.
- The marginality of the field.
- The multiplicity of roles and functions carried by individual staff.
- The significant time and cost factors incurred by part-time staff in taking up training opportunities.
- The tension between different providers of training courses, the practitioner versus the academic.

The east favours a more inclusive approach of training all those involved in the education of adults, in whatever agency, institution, or sector; and the west continues with its much more selective type of training according to the level and specialism of work. The reflection on a 'vast army of unpaid volunteers for whom adult education is their secondary professional concern' (Oglesby, 1991) would still be acknowledged as a valid one in both east and west Europe. There are, however, small signs that the issue is beginning to be recognized as a fundamental one.

> One of the common objectives concerns promoting 'a Europe of skills' of which one element must be improvements in the initial and continuing training of education staff.   (EC, 1989b)

Conclusion

The role of education for both halves of Europe is that it should enable people to learn; to encourage creativity; to inculcate flexible attitudes to changing situations, and to contribute to the general cultural development of the individual.

The victory has come as a cataract of events, almost overnight ... sparking off roaring enthusiasms. It must now give rise to earnest efforts to stabilise the emerging democracies by economic or financial co-operation and aid. The nations in the east need substantial economic assistance from the EC for the fledgling democracies to get settled. (Schmidt, 1990)

Adult education has always had a salient role in enabling people to learn about and cope with dramatic social, economic, and political changes but its role has been particularly interesting within Europe in recent years. It is likely to remain so up to the year 2000.

9

Enabling Learning: Raising the Profile of Staff Development. A Trainer's View

Lorna Unwin

By the end of this century, school leavers, FE students, graduates, adults in jobs and those returning to the labour force will all have an on-going record of their achievements, have produced action and training plans, be taking part in comprehensive job-related training and be developing transferable skills. In addition, all 18 year olds will be passing five GCSEs or possess an NVQ Level 1 and at least half of them will have an NVQ Level 3 or two A levels, and half of the employed workforce will also have an NVQ Level 2. The minority of teenagers who choose to leave school at 16 will only go into jobs with training and, like the majority who leave at 18, they will have at least £1000 to spend on training in the college or company of their choice. Thousands of women will have been persuaded to return to paid work, people aged over 50 will be valued in the workplace and anyone in a management position will have met the competence demands of the Management Charter initiative.

That vision of the future is distilled from various documents and statements produced in the late 1980s and early 1990s. If the rhetoric is translated into practice then Britain's economic prosperity is secure and her people will be reaching their full potential. In this chapter, I will examine that vision in the light of current industrial, educational and human resource realities. I will concentrate, in particular, on the demanding role which the vision allots to trainers and educationalists and advocate the need for a new nationally recognized professional organization whose membership would be open to anyone who has a responsibility for helping other people learn.

An uneasy partnership

The targets presented in the opening paragraph presuppose a close working relationship and a large degree of empathy between the relevant partners.

They also presume that each partner is healthy enough to play its specific role and understands exactly what is expected. The partners include educationalists and their institutions, employers and their training personnel, trades unions and professional associations, local and national agencies such as the TECs and their Scottish equivalents, Local Enterprise Companies (LECs); Chambers of Commerce; the NCVQ and its Scottish equivalent, SCOTVEC; national government as legislator and funder; and last but not least, the individual students and employees. To be effective, however, this relationship will have to operate within and ultimately clean up a climate polluted over the years by mistrust, envy, rumour and disrespect.

That climate is epitomized by the following viewpoints. Training is suddenly fashionable, wears new expensive clothes and appears to mock its underprivileged cousin, education, who is struggling to stay alive. The voice of training is dominant while education whispers in corridors, grateful if anyone stops by to listen. When the two meet, training plays bountiful host or, in aggressive mood, taunts education with examples from the latter's dismal record. Training is the *nouveau-riche arriviste*. An alternative view would see training as the working-class cousin who has never been allowed to mix properly with the other branch of the family.

Such images are easily constructed depending which cousin you wish to defend or castigate. Both training and education, however, share the same fate when scapegoats are needed to explain away the declining economic effectiveness of this country both at home and abroad. Deciding where the true blame should be laid for such decline is not the concern of this chapter nor is there need to spell out the massive capital investment not only in plant and machinery, but also in the quality and volume of its education and training provision which the country needs to make in order to begin to compare favourably with most of its foreign competitors and EC partners.

At the time of writing, it is patently obvious that the country's schools are desperately underfunded and that teachers are demoralized by constantly increasing professional burdens imposed from on high. This chapter does not, therefore, presume to apply its message to the school sector.

Extra funding would greatly help improve FE and HE and meet some of the training needs of industry. Such funding would almost certainly not, however, address the fundamental issues of the relative *status* of training and education within the community, their effectiveness in meeting both the individual client's and country's needs, and the establishment of meaningful partnerships leading to a sharing of expertise and mutual respect. In addition, funding *per se* would not throw light on the different cultures of education and training and the structures that divide them.

At the post-compulsory level, both education providers and industry must agree that each has an equally valuable role to play in enabling individuals to develop their full potential and that, whenever possible, that role must be shared. There are already examples of such partnerships, some of which have emerged through or been encouraged by national schemes such as PICKUP (mid-career updating) and REPLAN for the unemployed (lamentably wound up in 1991), both funded by the DES, the Royal Society of Arts (RSA) Education for Capability movement, and the Enterprise in Higher Education programme funded by the DE. At local and regional levels, partnerships have been forged between companies and colleges to cover specific occupational skills and to jointly provide NVQs. In the main, however, those partnerships perpetuate traditional lines of demarcation. Hence, management personnel will register with the polytechnic or university, while clerical and supervisory staff are likely to attend the local college of FE. Operative staff, if they are lucky, will receive their further training on the factory floor while carrying out their jobs.

On the face of it, there is a perfectly understandable reason for this educational hierarchy. HE provides the content and teaching required for management studies and so on down the line. This mirror-image of the education system imposed within a company structure depresses opportunities for staff to demonstrate their true potential and does little to encourage the concept of life-long learning. Furthermore, it would seem to work against the chance of creating a workforce that can adequately cope with and respond to the changing workplace with its increased use of new technology, growing demand for industrial and commercial inventiveness in terms of products and services and a switch to smaller numbers of full-time or 'core' workers supported by a larger cohort of part-time or sub-contracted labour. This need for 'flexible specialization' (FS) (Piore and Sabel, 1984) has major implications as Phillimore (1989) points out:

> Training policy is moving to the centre stage of political debate in many advanced industrialised countries. The FS debate is likely to reinforce this, implying as it does the potential of a renewed demand for high-level skills. If it proves to be the case that we are moving towards an FS regime, the implications for training could be profound for management and government. They would also provide a strong challenge to trade unions. For employers, the creation of a 'core' workforce has been accompanied by an increasing preparedness to provide resources for extensive retraining and upgrading of their workers' skills to ensure functional flexibility. However, as yet, most re-skilling (in Britain) has been add-on in nature and has not involved the definition of a new core-skill requirement, reflecting the pragmatic rather than strategic attitude of most firms in their skill requirements.

Phillimore's reference to high-level skills is echoed by Handy (1989) who has suggested that by the year 2000, at least 70 per cent of all jobs in Europe will require cerebral rather than manual skills and at least half of those will require the equivalent of a HE or professional qualification. Handy's predictions, and, in turn, the current rhetoric expounding the need for all employees to be flexible, do need to be viewed in the light of economic and social realities. Storey and Sisson (1990) remind us that the dynamic of changing work patterns must be kept in perspective:

... the much-touted 'core periphery' model is often mis-used to imply a generalised 'strategy' on the part of employers to create a more 'flexible' workforce. In fact, a not inconsiderable part of this recomposition of the labour force is accounted for by labour-supply factors rather than by policies on the demand side. For example, the Labour Force Survey in 1987 showed that only one in ten women with a part-time job had taken that job because they could not find a full-time one.

(Storey and Sisson, 1990)

Storey and Sisson also note that:

Although there was a substantial decline in manufacturing employment of around 40 per cent between 1978 and 1986, large-firm employment continues on a significant scale. In 1984 44.9 per cent of employees in manufacturing worked in establishments with 500 or more employees, and 44.7 per cent were employed by enterprises with 2000 and over employees. This level of concentration reflects the position as it was in the 1950s.

(Storey and Sisson, 1990)

Then there is the question of whether Handy's predictions apply to all newly created jobs or a select proportion. In the USA and Canada, the biggest growth areas of employment are fast food and cleaning. Such jobs, and many available in Britain too, involve a periphery army of reserve labour and not Handy's 'core'. At the time of writing, unemployment in Britain is rising sharply and there is talk of the Government re-introducing a version of the Community Programme which, rather than promote life-long learning or FS simply gives the unemployed tasks to keep them occupied albeit with a community face. This poses a continuing problem for anyone involved in the post-compulsory sector whether they are classed as educators or trainers. By believing in the rhetoric of life-long learning (and included here are currently fashionable concepts such as the Accreditation of Prior Learning, Access, core/generic skills), educators and trainers take on the responsibility themselves for empowering individuals whose real work choices may be extremely limited. The all-important debate about economic management and social justice can then be removed as the rhetoric takes over.

Given this demand for a 'better educated' workforce and the need for a strategic and holistic approach to training, there is a major omission in Phillimore's list of parties facing profound implications. I would add the training profession and both further and higher education who, working together with management, government and the trade unions, can help identify and create opportunities for the amount of learning and personal development implied.

Current partnerships between educational institutions and industry, hampered by problems of hierarchy and lack of holism, are further flawed by being largely based on the former servicing the needs of the latter. Some attempt has been made to encourage teachers at all levels to spend time working with the companies to which they will send their students on placement for work experience or after completion of their course. However, this is rare and it is often left to the learners to bridge the gap between the two distinct cultures. Furthermore, the influence which each side can have on the other is almost totally restricted to the narrowly defined objectives of single courses. Worse still, the fact that the focus of the learning is almost totally on the occupationally specific content required allows some staff on both sides of the divide to continue using traditional teacher or trainer-centred methods of delivery which are inappropriate both for the long-term needs of employers and the individual learners concerned.

Reclaiming the language of learning

There have been a number of reforming measures and philosophies which attempt to promote an atmosphere in which occupationally (academically) specific content, transferable skills and personal development are given equal prominence in the learning cycle. They range from the so-called pre-vocational programmes instigated by the Further Education Unit (FEU) from the late 1970s through to the RSA's Higher Education for Capability programme (1990). Reviewing its concept of vocational preparation, which sought to prepare young people for life roles rather than just paid work roles, the FEU (1987) stated that it should aim:

- to give young people basic skills, experience and knowledge;
- to help them assess their potential, to think realistically about jobs and employment prospects to optimize their employability;
- to develop their understanding of the working and social environment, both nationally and locally, so that they may understand the variety of roles possible for them to play as an adult member of society;
- to encourage them to become progressively responsible for their own personal development.

Compare the FEU view with RSA's 1990 assertion that:

> If students are given opportunities to be more responsible for their own learning, individually and with others, and to explore and explain the relevance of their studies to themselves and the society in which they live and work, they will develop their abilities to: acquire and apply knowledge; communicate ideas and information; listen to and collaborate with others in mutually planned activities; set achievable goals; assess the effectiveness of their actions; see both success and failures as opportunities for learning; be critical of and creative in their thinking and actions; take account of their feelings and intuition; reflect on their values.

The same message is seemingly coming from the employers, illustrated by these comments from Peter Slee of the CBI:

The common denominator of highly qualified manpower (sic) will, therefore, be the ability to think, learn and adapt. Personal transferable skills – problem-solving, communication, teamwork – rather than technical skills defined with narrow occupational ranges, will come to form the stabilizing characteristic of work. If higher education is to meet the needs of the economy and the individual it must seek actively to develop these generic core competencies that will in future define work.

(Slee, 1989)

Whether we are concerned with the 16-year-old school leaver seeking work, an undergraduate or FE student, or an adult already in or returning to paid work, there has been, for many years, a growing consensus that all should be nurtured as potentially autonomous learners who deserve and need far more than an input-based education and training system which uses force-feeding as its chief method of delivery. Who could oppose the laudable aims quoted in the extracts above? The problem is that for most people – and that includes employers, trainers, educationalists and often learners themselves – those ideas are still being dismissed, often for very genuine reasons. These include:

- *Fear* – Based on a shift in role from 'teacher' or 'instructor' mode to 'facilitator'.
- *Disbelief* – That a learner-centred/client-centred approach is workable given existing staffing ratios, accommodation, number of hours in the day and demands of examining bodies.
- *Lowering of standards* – Arising from the view that meaningful content disappears while individual learners become lost in a sea of abstract concepts.
- *Paper qualifications count* – Based on the continued widespread recruitment practices of employers and entrance requirements of educational institutions which demand 'official' evidence of ability.

For those of us who are sufficiently 'in the know' it is stimulating and, at times, almost evangelical to continue to refine our learner-centred vision of the world. We play the game and, in an attempt to further clarify the vision, constantly develop codewords and shorthand which serve to keep the rest of the world from joining in. This exclusiveness is not so much designed but often an unintended outcome of the structuring of academic discourse. Ironically, much of that private language consists of words and phrases which are meant to reflect a significant change in the approach to teaching and training styles, an approach that empowers the individual learner rather than concentrating control in the hands of the teacher. Those steering the changes talk of the importance of open learning, learner-centredness, recognizing experiential learning, accrediting prior achievement, peer and self-assessment, meeting individual needs and so on. Parallel to this pedagogical shift is massive curriculum change brought about by the introduction of competence-based vocational qualifications and educational content expressed as learning outcomes (see Chapter 14).

Thus the practitioner is faced with both an increasing number of new or refurbished policy initiatives and an accompanying plethora of pedagogical approaches. To survive in this changing landscape, practitioners at every level need to memorize an ever-lengthening glossary of acronyms and terminology.

All occupations have their own private language, as indeed do families, but usually this is employed to help people work together more easily and quickly and to create a sense of comradeship. There are three major problems with having an extensive and complex private language in the field of learning and personal development:

1. It creates exactly the sort of barrier to learning which most teachers and trainers agree should be dismantled.
2. There is a great danger that a thick veneer of sophistication is painted over what should be an essentially dynamic and free-moving set of processes which together enable people to learn in a vast range of settings and at many different levels.
3. It becomes increasingly harder for the fighting troops to both acquire and use that language in their own context as the inventors and disciples of the language and policies, who in the main are not frontline practitioners, increase its complexity and sophistication. To help and support practitioners and, significantly, to ensure that good practice is shared locally and nationally, attention must be given to the function, structure and funding of staff development for all practitioners from the workplace supervisor to the professor in higher education.

Raising the profile of staff development

Anyone with experience of the Youth Training Scheme (YTS) will be familiar with the admirable Design Framework which emphasized processes such as trainee-centred learning, reviewing and assessment leading to the development of both occupationally specific and transferable skills together with personal effectiveness. The employment-based trainers, workshop instructors and college lecturers who were faced with the challenge of putting the YTS framework into action received, at the most, a 16-day staff development programme (City and Guilds Youth Trainer's Award). Not only did that programme aim to shift people from a teacher-centred to a learner-centred style of delivery, it also had to train participants to complete newly introduced YTS documentation which included the recording of *103* core skills! A similar situation exists with the introduction of NVQs which require education and training professionals to grapple with Accreditation of Prior Learning (APL), work-based assessment and learners on individual programmes.

In addition to the massive pedagogical shift required for a learner-centred education and training system, the domino effect in terms of organizational structure is only just beginning to filter through. The much heralded 'learning organization' (Peters and Waterman, 1982; Garratt, 1987) demands a high degree of understanding about learning from all personnel responsible for training and managing others. A large manufacturing company in the Midlands which revamped its training policy by introducing NVQs discovered that once you allow your workforce to demonstrate their true potential you have to address the way in which the whole plant, including the shopfloor, is structured. For example, the traditional supervisor and chargehand have to be replaced by team leaders, and progression from operative to management level has to be more fluid (Unwin, 1991). Creative approaches to training which facilitate rather than prescribe learning will often reveal an uncomfortable 'can of worms' for any organization:

> The methodologies of action learning, self-managed learning and self-development became common by the early 1980s and the problem which then began to emerge was that of poor organizational performance – of sluggishness, an excess of bureaucracy and over-control, of organizations as straight jackets frustrating the self-development efforts of individual members and failing to capitalize upon their potential. The Learning Company is one in which learning and working are synonymous; it is peopled by colleagues and companions rather than bosses, subordinates and workers; and both the inside and outside of the company are continuously being searched and examined for newness – new ideas, new problems, new opportunities for learning. (Pedler *et al.*, 1989)

At the time of writing, the Lead Body for Training and Development has published its draft standards which will determine a range of trainer competencies to be expressed in subsequent NVQs for professionals in the field. There is talk of a further Lead Body being established for post-compulsory education which would set standards for teachers in FE and HE. While some educationalists will throw their hands up in horror at the thought of the competence movement getting its dirty hands on their 'profession', the standards are one way to concentrate minds upon the increasingly important role of the facilitator. Tragically, however, there is a real danger that the standards will only serve to further cement the existing divide between those who see their function as concerned with training and those who see their function as concerned with education. If only the Lead Body had been called the Lead Body for Enabling Learning and Personal Development, it could have acted as a national vehicle for bringing together *all* professionals concerned with helping others learn. In addition, and most importantly, it should be within the power of such a body to confer the coveted Qualified Teacher Status (QTS) on all professionals in the post-compulsory sector whether in adult education, FE or HE. Such a move would enhance and give improved status to the currently deficient pedagogic development of such professionals.

By coming together under the auspices of a joint, publicly funded body, professionals from all branches of education and training could share their expertise and learn from one another. Crucially, by representing the front-line practitioners, this body could insist on the necessary levels of support

required for staff development at all levels and across all sectors to understand and embrace new ideas and concepts. At the moment, staff development is desperately short and narrowly focused. In most universities and
polytechnics it is voluntary and restricted to one-day courses on using
information technology, time-management, and career-counselling, with
little or nothing on teaching skills or learning processes. In colleges of FE,
staff development is often reactive to events. In companies, far too many
trainers are still seconded to the training department for short periods before
being allowed to return to their 'real' jobs. This cursory attitude to the status
of training within companies is echoed throughout educational institutions,
where often the staff development office or sector is hidden away and staffed
by two or three individuals within organizations which can boast several
hundred full- and part-time staff. Comments from a TA survey of company
attitudes to trainer training are equally applicable to the education sector:

> Many of the companies participating in this survey reported that there
> were difficulties in providing a satisfactory career structure for specialist
> 'career trainers' because of the small size of the training departments
> involved ... More generally, companies seeking to make use of 'non-
> career trainers', whilst on secondment, also need to ensure that the
> training department is not perceived by potential recruits as a 'dead
> end' which removes other career options.   (TA, 1990)

There is much publicity given in this country to our appalling record,
vis-à-vis our foreign competitors, of the numbers of people who participate in
training and post-compulsory education, and to the woeful outcome in qualification terms of that participation. (NEDO/Training Commission, 1988;
Finegold and Soskice, 1988; NIESR, 1989). Little attention is given, however, to the equally lamentable state of our staff development provision for
the professionals on whom the country relies for the development of a
flexible, productive workforce of well-motivated individuals for whom life-
long learning is both a priority and a source of enjoyment. Funding for
training and post-compulsory education has been concentrated on volume,
buildings and staff salaries. In the case of government-sponsored programmes now controlled by the TECs, there is a move to output-based payments
for the numbers of trainees achieving NVQs. Yet money for the staff development of trainers, in both the public and private sectors, continues to be
scarce. It is usually a case of seeing whatever is left in the pot after all other
bills have been paid.

To return to the vision of this chapter's opening – there is increasing
pressure on the post-compulsory sector to not only drastically improve this
country's education and training record but to transform society's approach
to and concept of learning. To shoulder such a burden and achieve such
demanding targets, professionals in the field require much more support than
they currently receive. The Thatcher and Major governments have not
hesitated to legislate for structural, and even curriculum reforms in the
education sector, yet when it comes to employers' training policies and

practices, voluntarism has been the order of the day. Since the Industry Training Boards were abolished, report after report has shown that British employers invest very little in training compared with their foreign competitors and, when recession comes, training is often the first item to be cut.

The TECs, too, have been established under the banner of one-sided voluntarism – employers can choose to join the club, yet colleges have found they have no choice as TECs take control of their work-related funding. NVQs, despite massive investment of public funds in their design, development and publicity, are simply offered to employers on a take them or leave them basis. The content of NVQs was supposed to reflect the 'real' needs of employers, unlike previous vocational qualifications which were felt to be too theory-based and out of touch with the workplace. Ironically, this content is now being questioned by the very employers it was designed to serve. By pursuing a reductionist, functional-analysis model of curriculum design, NCVQ and the Lead Bodies who specify the national industrial standards on which NVQs are based, have encouraged the education-training divide to widen even further. Employers are finding that while NVQs serve their immediate on-the-job skills needs at operative level (Levels 1 and 2 in NVQ terms) they fail to develop the adaptable employee who has the potential for further and more knowledge-based training.

A major step in the right direction would be the establishment of a single government Department of Education and Training (Raggatt and Unwin, 1991). This would encourage symbiosis and common standards across the sectors. It would also give training the status it needs, a status it can never have while it is confined within one section of the Department of Employment. Without a joint department, there is no hope of bridging the vocational–academic divide which continues to fail both the country as a whole and generations of young people who leave school feeling inferior to their academic peers. The targets listed in the opening paragraph to this chapter are unachievable while ever the vocational–academic divide persists.

10

Competition, Collaboration, Communities: The Involvement of LEAs in Post-compulsory Education[1]

Alan Parker

Introduction

Are LEAs obsolescent in post-compulsory education? The immediate future is uncertain; except that things will not remain the same. Since a general election looms it is worth looking briefly at three scenarios.

Another Conservative victory could lead to more of the same – a reduced role for local government (removal of one tier in Shire Counties), circumscription of functions and further emphasis on devolved management and contracting out. TECs can expect an enhanced role, particularly in promoting the national extension of Training Credits – the FE 'voucher'. The demise of all local government is less likely, but direct involvement of LEAs in the management of educational institutions would be reduced to a rump.

Looking to the Future (Labour Party, 1990), promised to streamline local government by forming 'most purpose' authorities on the pattern of existing district councils, some of which would have to be enlarged. New regional authorities would be created, beginning with a Scottish Assembly followed by Wales and the English regions.

Although there may be some encroachment on existing county functions the intention is to 'transfer power from non-elected bodies and from central government – *not* from local councils'. Their merger of PCFC and UFC into a 'Higher and Continuing Education Council' would advise government on all post-18 education and allocate resources to institutions, including 'adult education colleges, WEAs, the Open University and the University of the Third Age'. TECs would be retained but they would be reformed to make them 'representative and accountable' including 'Trade unionists . . . women and representatives of the local council and educational providers.' These newly socialized TECs would be 'the local arms of Skills UK', another new national body to promote a 'training culture' to collect and disseminate labour market information and overcome barriers to improved training. The question of ownership and control of FE institutions was not addressed. They have not resisted incorporation of FE colleges, but Jack Straw suggested they would remain within LEAs, akin to the London Polytechnics under ILEA.

A hung parliament, narrow majorities or minority government would be most likely to produce something closer to the status quo. However, current processes of change and development have a momentum of their own that will tend to continue without further legislative intervention. A move to unitary authorities could remain on the agenda as all parties have some policies that imply this outcome. A Royal Commission or committee of enquiry could be a more likely device for advancing policy in these circumstances.

The complete confiscation of education from local authorities has superficial attractions but would bring practical and political complications. There are important residual functions that would not be attractive to commercial or voluntary interests (Statements of Special Educational Need, Grants for Education Support and Training, Student Awards, etc.). Most of these involve the local implementation of central policy and are closely controlled by delegated legislation; they involve detailed decision making and include hard cases. There is little praise for their efficient operation, which is largely invisible, but aggrieved and disappointed individuals can be troublesome. Because of historical differences in levels of activity and spending, the standardization involved in any central takeover would result in an unpopular levelling down of service, or an unacceptable increase in total cost – the unpalatable effect of either would have to be borne, politically or fiscally, at the centre. The proposed FE Funding Councils will test this, with the political gain of reduction in local taxation levels, which seemed to have been the prime factor behind the 1991 proposals.

There are benefits, therefore, in allowing unglamorous but necessary work to be absorbed by a locally elected body and pragmatism may yet defeat ideology. Local authorities will be further weakened by legal, fiscal and administrative devices rather than killed outright. They are still too useful as a cheap and convenient – if sometimes obstreperous – mechanism for implementing government policy.

To summarize, policy is likely to move in a similar direction whatever the overall shape of the political landscape. Differences will be of speed, emphasis and style rather than content. We may not be too far wrong either way, to look in detail at where reforms already set in motion will take us if current developments are allowed to work through.

The impact of the Education Reform Act

It has become fashionable to dismiss local authorities as a spent force. Much of this rests on a misunderstanding of the ERA both in its historical context and its likely future effect. Elizabeth Reid (1990) demonstrated cogently that

ERA represented a less dramatic change from previous practice in FE than in schools and was not without historical precedent. She shows that the 'loss' of the polytechnics and colleges to the PCFC was essentially similar to the transfer of the Colleges of Advanced Technology (CATs) to the university sector in the 1960s. In neither case was control relinquished willingly but, significantly, in neither case was the power of LEAs to provide advanced level work removed. Section 120 of the Reform Act gives the LEA an unrestricted power to provide any higher education it deems necessary.

Higher education

Paradoxically the ERA has removed the Secretary of State's control over approval of new HE courses. (One of the few actual reductions in DES powers.) The funding has gone to PCFC and with it the power to influence by resource allocation; although, as a relatively minor paymaster, this influence will be less in maintained colleges than amongst polytechnics. In times of extreme financial restraint this power is decisive; but the legislative framework does not preclude a recrudescence of HE in the maintained sector if circumstances change. Interestingly, other policies directed to stimulating a 'market' in education and training – notably the increased proportion of costs to be carried by tuition fees – could in the longer term encourage such an outcome.

Already some polytechnics and universities are 'contracting out' work – including the first year(s) of degree programmes – to FE colleges. There are obvious mutual advantages. The HE institution can meet expansion targets without overstretching staff or physical resources, but keeping higher first-degree and postgraduate work 'in house'. Building links with a network of feeder institutions can also help secure the flow of students from non-traditional sources who will be needed to maintain expansion against demographic trends. For the FE institution there are short-term benefits in maintaining or expanding income and volumes of work. The prestige of the institution can be enhanced and more highly qualified staff can be attracted. It is easier to support the academic viability of the part-time courses (Higher National Diplomas and some professional qualifications) previously classified as 'Advanced' but regarded as 'Further' rather than 'Higher' Education, and funded by the LEA, under ERA.

This last point is significant for two reasons. First the expanding need for such courses at convenient local colleges militates against the concentration of provision that has been a long-standing feature of central government HE policy. Secondly the reclassification of a very substantial quantity of former advanced courses means that the maintained sector's share of PCFC funding (less than 5 per cent in 1990–91) seriously understates its real participation in this level of work.

Colleges will also be keen to maintain their involvement in HE with an eye to longer term benefits. Demonstration of the ability to deliver the first part of HE courses cost effectively could lead in time to competitive bids to the PCFC for direct funding – undercutting the parent institution. Alternatively support for independently offered HE could be sought from the LEA (if better times return), commercial sponsors or TECs. With enhanced tuition fees the gap between income brought by each student and the lower unit costs of maintained colleges could be relatively small. From the institutional perspective this could be seen as a stepping stone from corporate status to membership of the 'HE club' (See Chapter 5).

Adult education

At the other end of the scale the patchwork of activity that takes place under the umbrella of 'adult education' (AE) was hardly addressed by the ERA. It cannot be said to have been untouched because changes in the management and funding of schools and FE colleges, where most of it takes place, have had considerable knock-on effects. LEAs themselves, compelled to reassess their role in relation to the bulk of their institutions, are in many cases also reviewing their approach to AE. It is difficult to generalize as the starting point varies considerably. Many of the former ILEA Institutes will continue as more or less independent units. Some other authorities which ran separate AE initiatives are developing non-statutory schemes to delegate greater financial and managerial autonomy. Where the use of school premises is important extra money has had to be diverted to AE to pay market rates to school governing bodies. This, and general budgetary pressure, has caused fees charged for AE to be increased; in some areas it is now close to becoming a self-financing service, and this will be reinforced by the 1991 White Papers (HMSO, 1991b).

There is an overlap between AE and other local authority services, e.g. library or recreational facilities; indeed some authorities administer AE as part of a leisure services department. There is also a substantial contribution to AE in the broadest sense by a wide range of voluntary bodies. The Workers' Education Association and the Women's Institute immediately spring to mind but a very wide range of clubs, societies and charitable organizations offer courses within their field of interest. In 1980 the Unit for the Development of Adult and Continuing Education found a significant latent demand for AE but a need for increased advice and guidance to help clients find appropriate provision. With the drift of policy tending to encourage greater diversity in an already fragmented area the organization of that advice could be an important area for development. The 1991 White Papers are silent on this; it is not seen as careers advice.

The role of the LEA: continuity and change

One of the greatest strengths of the LEA is its general responsibility for a specific population. Post-compulsory education embraces an expression of very broad social need. The LEA alone has the legal duty, and the practical capacity, to take a view of those disparate needs, taking into account both individual wants and the wider interests of the community, and to allocate public resources to meet them. The exercise of broad, but locally and individually sensitive, discretion requires democratic accountability at a level that central government cannot provide. Private or voluntary agencies lack the scope and legitimacy of an elected body and, whilst they can carry out specific and closely defined functions, decisions on relative priorities, the type and level of service to offer, and final accountability for its delivery needs an elected body.

ERA explicitly gives LEAs this planning, monitoring and public account-ability role with regard to further education, alongside its power to provide adult education directly. It is charged with consulting and taking account of the interests of other providers and consumers in exercising its functions. It is for the LEA to assess the overall situation, take cognisance of what is otherwise provided and fill in the gaps – whilst balancing its own budget. This is again not greatly different from the 1944 Act. LEAs were then charged to *secure* adequate provision taking into account the contributions of private and voluntary schools. This 'gap filling' is a necessary function if the disparate elements that make up the totality of provision are to be made to function like the 'system' we pretend to have. However, the incorporated FE colleges will break the link to the local democracy if the 1991 proposals are enacted: LEAs will be specifically excluded from representation on their governing bodies.

Recent developments

Training credits

Training Credits were launched as an idea in March 1990 via a 'prospectus' inviting TECs to bid for funding to run pilot schemes. Willing participation of the relevant LEA(s) was made a condition of the bids. At the end of August 11 pilot schemes were approved to begin in April 1991 to run for 2 years. The 'credit' itself was to be a document with a cash value in the hands of 16+ school leavers intending to enter the labour market. It could be used by young people to buy part-time training and as a lever to persuade employers to support them. Unlike previous youth training initiatives which were launched as (more or less) fully formed national schemes, little was said about mechanics. The government specified the end 'To revolutionize atti-tudes to training in this country . . . to excite young people . . . and to raise the amount and quality of training provided by employers' (DE, 1990) and chose the vehicle – TECs – but the means, apart from the credit principle, were left entirely open.

Control of a small amount of general FE funding by TECs (in addition to the YTS and ET schemes they initially took over from the TA) could clearly be the thin end of the wedge. Extension of Training Credits, from a 10 per cent pilot scheme to a universal voucher system encompassing all public subsidy to post-school education and training, as now proposed, could be a vehicle for 'privatizing' FE. TECs would be responsible for letting contracts, and incorporated FE colleges would take their place among existing private providers. But there are flaws.

First it would be a spurious market because the 'customers' would be using a 'currency' that was neither real nor their own. The necessity of public subsidy is not questioned, but when that subsidy is expressed as a cash value and bestowed on individuals how are the very considerable training costs differentials to be accommodated – particularly when they do not necessarily correlate with the eventual earning power associated with the occupation in question?

Second, *who* is the customer – the trainee or employer? The public subsidy is given to the individual but employers are expected to participate using their own money; but if they are themselves training providers they could charge their own employees. Can the first employer of a young person be expected to stand proxy for the broader interests of future employers of an increasingly mobile labour-force? There is a dichotomy between the need to increase the quality and volume of training undertaken whilst exercising necessary economic planning, and the likely outcome of an unrestrained market in Training. The Association of Metropolitan Authorities (AMA) has argued that there is:

> ... an overlap of interest of employee and employer in VET [that] is the key to reconciling the perceived conflict between economic needs and individual aspiration ... Providing that the employer is not burdened with the full costs of training and the state plays an appropriate part, there is scope for creative partnership. (AMA, 1990a)

It is not self-evident that feeding an indiscriminate subsidy into a synthetic market where the role of employer and employee are ambiguous, and possibly in conflict, is the best way to create that partnership.

Germany is often held out as having vocational education systems that the UK should emulate. In 1989 a party of LEA elected members and employees visited the Federal Republic and reported:

> The AMA group was impressed by the *sense of commitment* of employers and trainers to a system developed since the war using many of the terms and principles of vocational qualification from the nineteenth and earlier centuries. The *statutory underpinning* seemed to be both an expression of this commitment and a means of perpetuating it ... Bayer (one of the companies visited) devoted 3 per cent of its total wage bill to training. We also noted that construction firms pay a training levy of 2 per cent. In what we observed, there plainly was an *ethos that holds training important*. There is a kind of 'training culture', an assumption that training is automatically part of most paid work. (AMA, 1990b)

It is painfully clear that such a 'training culture' does not yet exist amongst the generality of the UK workforce or employers. Official reports, much quoted and stretching back to the last century, have repeatedly made the point. Exhortation has not produced the necessary change in attitudes, and statutory measures have not worked – or have been found difficult and not tried (e.g. the provisions for universal day release to County Colleges in the 1944 Act echoing that of 1918, were finally repealed in 1988 without having been implemented).

The language used by ministers in launching the initiative demonstrates that Training Credits should be a means of changing attitudes as much as a vehicle for delivering a public subsidy to training. However, the very lack of that ethos could be a major factor working against its success. In so far as pilot schemes are restricted in scope and have a value conditional on the type of training sought they will tend to be perceived by trainees as no more than window dressing for the existing system; but as the value and freedom attached to the credit become more real it will become correspondingly more likely that 'deadweight' and popular, cheap provision leading to lucrative employment will soak up the already constrained public subsidy. Expensive and socially necessary training could then be left underfunded and in a spiral of decline.

Student support

The debate on student support has been focused largely on full-time students in HE. It is not necessary to rehearse the grants/loans debate here, but there are a number of ways in which the fallout from recent changes is likely to affect students in FE. The changes in regulations that have restricted students' access to housing benefit and supplementary benefit during the long vacation can bear more harshly on students ineligible for mandatory awards. They are also affected by the greater restrictions on the use of the '21 Hour Rule' relating to part-time study. The so-called 'access funds' given to institutions to compensate individual students will be inadequate to meet the hardship created by the loss of benefits; let alone help to provide the genuine extension of access that the agreed general policy requires. The power of LEAs to make discretionary awards would be an appropriate alternative source of funding – if authorities had the funding to help more students.

However, these budgets are being squeezed from two directions. Increased demand from students is meeting reduced budgets and the exercise of a discretionary power is inevitably of a lower priority than the discharge of statutory duties. The local government finance system also acts to increase the pressure. The assessment of the national need to spend in any year begins from the actual expenditure in the previous one. Thus if budgets are cut to meet a short-term cash shortage, central government assumptions about the 'need to spend' tend to be similarly depressed.

The next steps

British HE and FE policy has a history of incremental and evolutionary development, with reform adding to and modifying what exists. Further changes are unlikely to break this rule. There is certainly room for rationalization, particularly for the general-purpose FE colleges which sit at the centre of vocational education and training.

Rationalization

Typically (although the diversity of the sector is such that typicality is a dubious concept) such a college includes:

(a) 16–19 year olds continuing full-time education who could equally well be doing similar courses in schools;
(b) 16+ school leavers pursuing vocational courses part time whilst in employment or full time, through choice or because employment is unavailable;
(c) 18+ students on higher professional or academic courses – again full or part time, many of whom could find similar provision in polytechnics;
(d) older adults on similar courses, or pursuing leisure interests or involved in re-training or skills updating.

Within this pattern funding is a mixture of local authority formula funding with free tuition to full-time 16–19 year olds; nominal fees for part-time courses paid for by individuals or employers; full-cost provision for industry; and central government schemes via the TA or TECs. From 1991 Training Credits will fund some students on mainstream courses at full cost using central government funds (with some employer top-up) paid via TECs. This complex matrix cannot neatly be divided and certainly cannot be split by purpose between 'vocational', 'leisure' and 'academic' – as almost any course can be pursued for any of those reasons. Open learning, modularization, credit transfer and the expansion of client-centred approaches, will make distinctions by 'course' increasingly irrelevant, if not impossible.

However, some form of rationalization is badly needed. The accretion of a series of partial funding and planning mechanisms over the past decade has left colleges hamstrung by a plethora of complex bureaucratic requirements that impede rather than promote the responsiveness they were individually designed to achieve (AMA, 1990a). The prime example is the conflict between the 3-year rolling development plan that has to be agreed between the LEA and the Department of Employment; and the planning exercise the LEA must carry out to operate its formula funding scheme. Training Credits will cut across both funding mechanisms. LEAs have been accused of constraining their institutions, first polytechnics and now FE colleges. However, it has more often been central government interference that has been at the root of the problem. Prior to the loss of polytechnics, LEA control had produced the cost-effective expansion required by government that the universities had been unwilling or unable to deliver. As Reid (1990) has argued:

> It is ironic that in their recently published report on the polytechnics, HMI attributed some of these achievements to the Polytechnics themselves. In the debates about the preservation of the unit of resource versus increased access that were an annual feature of the NAB round, it was the boldness and determination of the LEA members which secured the expansion of provision, often against the advice of those who headed the institutions they maintained.

Planning

The idea of planning on the basis of predicted labour market need is now well established, and the principle of institutional autonomy within formula funded resourcing is also likely to survive any change of government. The key question then is who will plan and who will control the resource allocation.

The resources to be distributed will be public money raised by taxation. With Labour or Lab/Lib alliance it will be distributed by an LEA. The Conservative alternative might be TECs with some residual monitoring and oversight by central government or an agency under its control. This could be quite attractive looked at from the top with central government channelling money through 82 TECs plus the Scottish LECs contracted to implement *its* policies rather than 125 LEAs with some independent revenue raising powers and political commitment to policies of their own.

However, as has been argued above, it may be difficult for them to dispense entirely with some sort of locally elected body to mop-up residual functions. By definition such a body needs broadly defined powers which can then be exercised creatively. By the same token there is no guarantee that the TECs, once established, will meekly comply with central direction. They are already expressing dissatisfaction with their constrained role and inadequate funding. In some areas at least, local authorities are establishing good working relationships with their TEC and could come to exert significant influence. Rather than losing power locally, LEAs could secure a more significant role with respect to former TA functions than they have hitherto enjoyed. The need for coordination of planning is made more urgent by the 1991 proposals where 16–19 provision, and adult participation, could be in opted out schools, City Technology Colleges, LEA sixth forms, incorporated sixth form colleges *and* FE colleges with no local mechanism for coordination.

Careers guidance

One target for TEC expansion has been the careers service. It is a statutory LEA service which is nevertheless within the remit of the Department of

Employment, not the DES. It sits between schools, other HE/FE provision and employers but sees itself as owing a principal loyalty to the individual client. Currently funding is channeled to LEAs via an element in the general Revenue Support Grant which is overseen by DES, but there is also a specific grant, 'the Strengthening Scheme' (linked to levels of youth unemployment) which is directly controlled by the Department of Employment. The role of the service is important, as has been shown by its involvement in the development of Training Credit pilots, because greater reliance on market mechanisms for regulating education and training requires more and better advice being available to the consumer. It is here that the independence of the careers service is likely to become more important. Some fear that the take over by TECs advocated by the Confederation of British Industry (CBI) amongst others and foreshadowed in the 1991 White Paper (HMSO, 1991b) could lead to the principle being abandoned in a crude attempt to direct labour for the benefit of employers.

Work-related FE

In November 1990 it was announced that the money for 'Work-Related Further Education' (WRFE) (some £100m annually) controlled by the Department of Employment would pass to TECs. This cash was originally taken from the Rate Support Grant and given to the MSC and formed the basis for planning agreements between the TA and LEAs. With the demise of the TA there was little doubt that the cash would be transferred to TECs. Initially, TECs will merely take over the administration of the existing scheme. This was a disappointment to those who had lobbied for TECs to be given much greater flexibility to use the money to influence LEAs or buy training elsewhere. There will probably be continuing pressure to allow TECs more latitude in the use of this funding.

Because LEAs rely on the WRFE contract to provide a proportion of the General Colleges Budget (GCB) within their funding formulae, loss of this guaranteed funding would cause difficulties. Most authorities could not replace such a sum from the poll tax or its successor and simply to deduct it from the GCB would drive the unit or resource below any reasonable estimate of cost. The only alternative would be to reduce college target enrolments thus protecting unit funding. However, it would not be clear which areas of provision should be reduced and in any event the signal to colleges would run counter to the overall policy thrust towards increased participation.

A more rational approach, certainly in the medium term, would be a conflation of the various schemes and mechanisms into a coherent approach to planning and resource allocation. Any national successor to the Training Credit pilots would be at the centre of such arrangements and its overall character would be determined by the nature of the compromise between the 'market' approach they embody, and the 'planned' elements in the system currently represented by WRFE contracts and formula funding. One possible approach would be to channel all public subsidy for part-time provision through TECs via a Training Credit system with the redemption value of credits being a control mechanism determining the level of subsidy to different employers and types of training. The responsibility for all full-time provision could remain with the LEA, to fund students on both academic and vocational courses by formulae. This could go hand in hand with a bringing together of FE and school sixth form provision, fulfilling the current drift of convergence expressed through TVEI and other curricular reform, tertiary colleges, and proposals to offer part-time work in schools.

This would produce a system much closer to those in a number of European countries (e.g. France and Italy) where full-time academic and vocational education for young people is available in a range of institutions within the common framework of the Baccalaureate. If at the same time FE colleges were given corporate status the LEA, TEC and PCFC could become the main customers of colleges on an equal footing.

Corporate status

Much has been made of the issue of corporate status for FE colleges. Arguably formula funding, delegation and the ability to set up college companies can provide all the autonomy that a college might need (see Chapter 6). Continued maintained status can also offer certain benefits to institutions – a financial guarantor of last resort, a source of technical advice on a range of issues and a source of help in obtaining land, buildings and planning consent when expansion is required. From the point of view of the LEA, corporate status will now make little difference. The distinctions between the corporate London Polytechnics (both within ILEA and those responsible to more than one LEA) and those maintained by a single LEA were neither significant nor obvious to the casual observer prior to the 1988 reforms. There is even less reason to suppose that corporate status, *of itself*, will have more than symbolic importance.

However, it would release the LEA from the final responsibility as the owner of its colleges and free it to seek a consistent level of resourcing across all full-time provision for young adults. It might also open the way to a more direct contractor/client relationship between the LEA and FE institutions. This could have attractions for the LEA as well as the institutions. Apart from the tendency to make a virtue of necessity there is potentially greater freedom in using purchasing power to influence an independent provider than in attempting to control an institution for which you have legal responsibility without executive power. There is evidence that a number of LEAs are already looking critically at the functions that they have (and in particular those that they are most likely to keep) with a view to establishing more appropriate ways of working.

This is also being influenced by a broader reappraisal of the functions of elected members. One report of the Audit Commission (1990) focused on the split between policy making and strategic planning which are regarded as proper functions of elected members; and day-to-day management and decision making which should be left to officers. This analysis also attacks the bureaucratic model of both management and decision making that has traditionally been associated with local authorities. It is not difficult to see that as well as requiring a smaller cheaper organization, a slimmed down LEA might also be able to take a more active role in the development of policy and innovation and in quality assurance once relieved of detailed responsibility for day-to-day delivery of the service. It can further be argued that local councillors can be more effective as advocates on behalf of their constituents and promoters of their interests if they are not personally implicated in the detailed decisions that may be the cause of complaint.

Conclusion

Predicting the future at a time of rapid change is difficult when events tend to overtake journalistic deadlines. The longer timescales associated with book production make it even more likely that much of the foregoing will have been borne out or disproved by the time it appears in print. However, I suggest that if local government survives and retains an interest in education it will continue to exert influence on the post-compulsory phase.

Note

1. This chapter was completed before the announcement that FE and sixth form colleges were to be removed from LEA control. There have been minor amendments made by the editor. Events have overtaken it but in the view of the author and the editor the analysis remains pertinent. Much will depend on how far the amending legislation resolves the contradictions identified above, which will be crucially affected by the timing and outcome of the general election.

(C)
Prospective:
Views on Key Issues

11

Access: Growth, Outreach and Openness

Ian McNay

The E factors

Expansion has been almost ever present in post-compulsory provision since the Second World War. Changes in the basis of collection and presentation of statistics make detailed time-series comparisons difficult but, at a general level, that thesis can be defended. Different sectors have dipped at times – the universities in the early 1950s after the post-war boom and in the early 1980s in self-imposed restraint to defend the unit of resource; colleges of education in the 1970s after the ironically titled 1972 White Paper *Education: a Framework for Expansion*; FE with the collapse of apprenticeships and day release in the early 1980s; and AE in harmony with economic cycles or in response to fee rises, whether relating to imposition of VAT on some provision or provoked by constraints on local government finance. AE is the only sector now smaller than in the 1970s; the general trend is upwards.

This growth has rarely matched expectations or plans. In HE expansion immediately after the Robbins Report in 1963 was faster than predicted; in the 1970s projected student numbers for 1981 were constantly revised down, eventually by over 200,000. Because of reduction in the size of the 16–18-year-old cohorts, a drop in numbers in FE was confidently predicted for much of the 1980s but stubbornly refused to appear, to justify the planned reductions in staffing budgets. The basis of projections of student numbers is often difficult to understand. The factors that moderated the potential impact of demographic trends for 18-year-olds on entrants to higher education – e.g. a shift in class profile and more students from mature age groups – do not seem to have been applied to FE. Projections for HE ignore the effect of the value of the student grant and trends in employment, which undermines their validity immediately.

Government has moved from considering closure of HE institutions to projecting growth of home student numbers in HE by just under 500,000 by AD 2000 (HMSO, 1991c). Those figures too, are suspect: compare the growth

Table 11.1   Actual growth 1987–89 compared with projected growth 1989–2000

	Actual growth 1987–89 per cent	Projected growth 1989–2000 per cent
Full-time/Sandwich first and subsequent degree	9.5	70.6
Full-time postgraduates	14.5	14.3
All part-time	10.3	25.0

in 1987–89 with projected growth 1989–2000 in three categories in Table 11.1.

It seems that the full-time front-end model of HE persists in planners' minds despite recent realities and the reasonable assessment of the future impact of government policy, particularly over finance of both student maintenance and capital building.

Expansion of provision has not been uncontested. It is challenged by defenders of *excellence*. The 'more means worse' sloganists believed in limits to the 'pool of ability' among the population. For them excellence meant élitism. More recently there has been resistance, often token, from those pressured by the three Es of *economy, efficiency, effectiveness*. There is a belief prevalent among ministers that the first two can be pursued *ad infinitum* without effect on the third. The competitive drive of some polytechnic directors, and the FE tradition of elasticity to accommodate demand gave the belief substance. Though resources were cut, and student numbers increased, no leader of an institution, until recently, would say that quality had been affected: it was always *going* to be, soon, but no one would be the first to admit that it *had* been because of the impact on the institution's image. The stand by the UGC and its institutions post-1981 held only until it saw loss of influence to other sectors looming as they raced ahead in total student numbers and gained in government and student eyes by an image of responsive, relevant entrepreneurialism and flexibility. Yet there are limits to 'more means cheaper' and one of the key debates to the end of the century is *when* 'cheaper' means 'worse'.

Expansion has not satisfied campaigners for *equality*; indeed the statistical evidence on the pattern of expansion fuelled the debate on access. Government had a simple equation: because more people entered HE it was, *ipso facto*, 'more accessible to people from *all* sections of society' (HMSO, 1991c, emphasis added). Some FE college principals when challenged on access use a similar argument and point to crowded classrooms, high SSRs, and staff burdened with more administration and worse conditions of service as a defence against doing more. The argument, however, is not only about expansion – doing more – but about being different to attract a different balance of participants.

Table 11.2 The percentage of school leavers with at least one A/H level pass in 1988

Principality	Male	Female
England	19.0	18.4
Wales	16.7	19.1
Scotland	32.0	39.8
Northern Ireland	23.4	29.8

Source: *Social Trends* 1991, Table 3.13.

Patterns of growth and participation

Some of the shifts in balance, developed during the 1980s and continuing to the end of the century, are slowly emerging from statistical studies, which also puncture some of the myths promoted by government and others. In the mid-1980s, for example, the proportion of male students gaining the equivalent of five C grades at 'O'level was at best static and at times declined slightly. At the same time there was a flight of home male applicants to university through UCCA. No boom there! Women now form a clear majority in most sectors of post-16 provision except day-release students in FE and graduate students; in AE they are dominant. This is despite deterrent and discriminatory factors:

(a) the personal safety issue in evening attendance;
(b) poor public transport when women have harder access to private cars;
(c) lack of child-minding provision;
(d) the persistence with traditional examination patterns;
(e) selector bias.

In 1980 the proportion of women entrants through UCCA matched the proportion of applicants; by the end of the decade entrants were three per cent below applicants. For men, of course, the figure was reversed. Nor was it solely pressure on popular arts subjects: the UCCA silver jubilee report showed that female applications had risen nine-fold in engineering, entrants only by seven-fold.

The dominance by women is greater in the nation regions of the UK than in England (Table 11.2). There is fertile ground there for education sociologists to explore. The Scottish figures make a case for staged progression at 16+ which AS levels might provide elsewhere in the UK. For Northern Ireland the high overall figure can be used to defend single-sex grammar schools, religious control and segregation, or the use of deprivation as an incentive to escape via education.

The performance of women can be linked to two other issues at 16–18. Despite government sponsorship of private schools by the Assisted Places

Scheme, the growth in candidates with good A levels has been in the despised and derided comprehensives. Government has not published comparative figures now for some years, perhaps because objective reality does not accord with their ideological needs. The other link is to the collapse of students of maths at A level, and, to a lesser extent, Physics and Chemistry. Again, this is less of a problem in Scotland with its different tradition and wider post-16 curriculum. Women have always been less inclined to maths – the percentage studying A level being roughly half that for male students, so their increasing share of a cohort would reduce *proportionate* figures. However, the *absolute* numbers across the sexes are down. While the overall numbers taking and passing A levels increases, numbers in maths have declined by around 10 per cent per year for several years. Computer studies is also in decline. First-generation post-16 students tend to favour arts and social science (this is true at degree level, too) and the problem is now spiralling since a shortage of good teachers will make things worse.

This has significant implications for HE in science, engineering, architecture, even economics, and for the supply of highly qualified personnel to industries seen as the key to economic recovery. The trend will not be reversed soon, nor without substantial resource investment, not only to compensate at the point of entry to HE for shortfall in applicants but, as with programmes in New York to attract black and hispanic applicants, by seeing lower secondary levels as a key influence on students' later decisions.

HE needs to reach out to help at those levels in making science attractive, exciting and accessible. There are 'image' problems to tackle on a wider basis to help change science from being seen as an impersonal, dangerous, polluting, destructive force. There the responsibility should not be loaded onto education as has been done in allocating blame for economic failure. Others must take a lead.

If there has been a shift in gender balance, there has also been a shift in age balance. The majority of students in both FE and HE are now over 21 on entry; the average age of Open University undergraduates went up from 33 to 35 between 1985 and 1989; the University of the Third Age is thriving. AE has long been used to serving such students and the experience there would be a useful study for many staff in other sectors faced with increasing numbers, particularly when they have a purchasing power through paying their own fees at near-economic rates. They have a life experience on which they will have reflected to form views. Any teaching must recognize this: as valid learning, not to be dismissed as merely anecdotal; as a point of departure for judging the relevance of course content; and, positively, as a resource to draw on and to learn from. Older students have often been seen as disruptive because they are less compliant, less ready to accept unchallenged *ex cathedra* statements, and more critical of poor environmental conditions and resource support. One retired university registrar told me that she would always give preference to younger students because a homogeneous group was easier to deal with and, anyway, others had had their chance. Such attitudes are slowly changing as mature students prove themselves against their younger competitors.

Elsewhere, problems may be of resource: there is considerable demand from retired people for building trade skills for DIY, but wet areas for brickwork projects are used for 'mainstream' courses. Where do priorities lie? The question of assessment is also important. Older students – and by that I encompass almost anyone over 35 – are fearful of exams as the physical demand of speed writing for long periods and the mental demand of rapid recall from short-term memory become less easy to meet. The nature of student support and counselling also changes for older students whose life crises are less likely to include glandular fever and first love than child care, redundancy, incipient arthritis or senile parents.

The third group who have featured in recent expansion of student numbers are those from families where English is not the first language. Numbers in universities from beyond the EC are slowly returning to the levels prevalent before full-cost fees were introduced in 1981. Elsewhere that is not the case in spite of recruitment drives. It seems likely that with a buoyant 'home' market and with home students bringing near-economic fees with them as part of their grant, the pressure to recruit such overseas students will diminish, at least at undergraduate level. There has, though, been significant growth in students from within the Common Market and this is likely to accelerate after 1992 as part of the freer market and as students from the European mainland seek shorter courses than those at home with the bonus of reinforcing their English language skills. The third element in this group is the intake from the ethnic minority communities in the UK. Students from such groups are over-represented in HE relative to their presence in the community at large, and, presumably, this applies to feeder courses in schools and FE post-16. That generalization does not apply to all groups: Bangladeshis under-participate, as do Afro-Caribbean men – though not women who out-perform their men by a remarkable ratio of 17:1.

This record is not without its down side. UCCA figures show that for universities the proportion of black entrants is half that of applicants, with a commensurate balance among polytechnics and colleges, and reports on admissions criteria for some London teaching hospitals and for dentistry in Glasgow make shameful reading. Students from the Asian communities tend to apply for professional courses where the competition for entry is greater but then so, it appears, is their commitment, and their performance, in general, outscores the white indigenous population. Again, institutions have had to adapt, with varying degrees of willingness.

Dietary and other observances need catering for. Examples in a variety of courses need to be drawn from diverse cultures and care is needed with language, as was true with women, even if not to the lengths of 'political correctness' now oppressing the USA. The common culture of the Robbins Report can no longer be assumed, and a new multi-source synthesis needs to be developed by open recognition of and esteem for existing differences.

The groups consistently under-represented in post-compulsory education are the working class and the unemployed – who, since classification is by occupation, are necessarily *déclassé*.

The latter group forms a fourth stratum below those used in Chapter 9:

they attend training centres on a succession of 'schemes' before rejoining the massaged statistics. Some experimental approaches under the now guillo- tined DES Replan scheme have been successful within their limits but few of the unemployed see education as relevant to their needs: many of them rejected it as soon as possible when in the 'compulsory' age group. This is an indictment of the providers of education as much as of the non-students themselves.

The working class, too, do not see FE and HE as appropriate or accessible. Statistics here are scanty and universities are perhaps over-criticized because UCCA *does* produce them. In spite of growth, the proportion of students from 'lower' classes entering universities declined over the 1980s, especially when competition was most intense. The 1987 Household Survey suggested that participation from Group E in HE overall had halved – from 2 per cent to 1 per cent in 10 years. Such students' attainment may understate their ability since they are less likely to have a supportive home background or a well- resourced and staffed school when schools mirror their catchment neighbour- hood. This may, like the gender issue above, be more an issue in England with its class consciousness than in the other countries of the UK. If, how- ever, the recent surge in qualified school leavers continues and is accelerated by the bottoming out of the demographic decline in 16–18-year-olds, such marginal students may be less inclined to continue study. The 'sponsorship' they are offered by staff when numbers are low will be progressively (or rather *not* progressively!) withdrawn. That may be true for the other groups treated here, too. Indeed, the recent growth that has drawn them in may simply be because of a slackening in demand from traditional students.

Growth brings problems in itself: pressure on resources, the risk of anomie, support spread more thinly. One result can be a higher rate of non- continuing students. This was so with the universities in the second half of the 1980s where the October headline figures for growth in intake were not reflected in returns to the Universities' Statistical Record for 'finally reg- istered' students at the end of December. With 'non-traditional' students the likelihood is even greater. Smithers, reported in *The Higher* (16 August 1991), suggests that 65 per cent of those who continue in education after 16 gain no qualifications. In the USA, there may be mass access, but there is also mass exodus – the 'revolving door' syndrome. Half of those on four-year courses do not complete within six years, and over nine out of ten of those on two-year programmes drop out (DES, 1989a).

Further growth needs more resource to give students support. It needs a restructuring of teaching programmes to allow regular achievement of targets which are seen as reachable from the outset – access students laugh when asked to picture themselves in gowns and hoods at graduate ceremonies; they *don't* laugh at the idea of testing the water (and themselves) on first-year modules (Curry, 1989). It needs, also, a review of teaching and learning processes, so that staff develop skill in the one and students in the other. Too often, at present, both are assumed to be innate in those who choose to carry labels – 'lecturer' or 'student'. Teachers need to be less didactic and more developmental; students need to learn not only by themselves and for themselves, but together working with and for others – as they will be expected to do in work situations.

These issues will be all the more urgent if access is to be a reality, since the needs of access students, and of those who support them, are even greater. That depends how you see the future.

Alternative futures

It seems likely that demand for further and higher education will continue to rise. Reforms to curriculum and exams at 16+ led to a 5 per cent leap in those reaching the basic threshold of five acceptable grades at this level. More children now have parents who have been through HE and so normative expectations have shifted, as may the social composition of successive cohorts as the different rates of change in birthrates by class work their way through. Lower fertility came first to the middle classes which may account for sluggish qualification rates in the 1980s; the balance later redressed itself. The withdrawal of benefits from those aged under 18 provided a stick to drive the more reluctant back into the classroom with, perhaps, incidental impact on qualification rates. The increase, since the 1960s, in participation in FE and HE as part of an initial phase may, however, mean that there will be fewer older students who feel the need to compensate for lack of initial qualifications. This could well be compensated for by those seeking second qualifications, professional updating or career change.

The need for qualified personnel will also increase, though the main deficit seems likely to continue to be at technician level and equivalent and at supervisory and junior management levels rather than anything more high-flying. With fewer young people feeding in to the workforce, retention and retraining of older staff will take on increased importance.

The question is: can this demand from both sides be met by an 'industry' which is under-capitalized, in need of plant modernization, with an ageing professional workforce and a barely competitive salary structure, especially for support staff? It seems likely that private funds will increasingly be sought, but these have a price not only in loss of control of the product to those commissioning it but also in displacing 'core' activities. There are already cases of undergraduate classes being cancelled or rescheduled because lecture theatres were booked for profitable conferences or high-priced professional updating courses. Access provision is likely to be squeezed out in some places since 'standard' students are so much easier to deal with. If there are enough of them, why look further? In the words of one senior university administrator on an access consortium: 'After all, if I admit an access student, it means excluding a good applicant.' He was pressing for examinations on access courses to allow easier equivalence with A levels, at least in stratifying students by achievement. The conflict between the access philosophy and the exam philosophy may be resolved by 'general NVQs' (HMSO, 1991b).

Without growth there may be no room for new groups of entrants, so that growth has to be beyond that which matches patterns of demand from mainstream students. Three institutional strategies may emerge. With the commodification of education which Schuller notes (Chapter 3), there is a market analogy to each.

The first could be called the Harrods approach. It was anticipated long ago by the Conference of University Administrators (1978). Prestige institutions have weathered the demographic depression and can now confidently await an upsurge in traditional clients among whom they can pick and choose. Any shift in product profile in HE is likely to be at graduate level – it has been the fastest growth area for the past decade – and in bespoke development for senior professional staff. So, customers/products are re-cycled, or called in for maintenance or, like computers, upgrading. At 16 + the rise in A level students could save small uneconomic sixth forms with pretensions from the financial audit axe and even allow them to exclude those they had accommodated in harder times who only wish to re-sit exams. They could then narrow their range of activity and concentrate on a specialist clientele.

The second option is the supermarket analogue. A range of products is developed, packaged and 'marketed':

(a) modular courses offer a pick 'n' mix approach building into a diploma in twelve regular parts;
(b) part exchange offers are available through credit transfer schemes or accreditation of prior learning;
(c) brand loyalty is encouraged by reduced study time at master's level for one's own graduates, and by alumni associations;
(d) student loans introduce an h.p. element – 'study now, pay back later';
(e) other colleges are 'franchised';
(f) mail order and self-service models are available through open and distance learning;
(g) prospectuses often look like travel brochures or mail order catalogues.

There are even specialist consumer publications such as *Which Degree?* Access courses can be seen as loss leaders, a 'come-on' which guarantees entry to linked courses. Some courses even have special offers of supplementary grants, absolutely 'free'! I could extend into mergers, asset stripping, board room salaries, but the point is made. There is a risk that, under financial pressure, the cheaper, cheerful and competent may cut corners and standards; that customer care, an essential element of marketing, *could* be neglected and that the 'free market', which never existed anyway, becomes a flea market where things of established value are neglected, left to rust and dust, and displaced by the latest gizmo and gimmick. We must hope that the plastic bags advertising 'quality and service' or 'the good costs less at –' continue to be justified.

The third model is the corner shop – 'open all hours'. It may be, as David Bradshaw (Chapter 5) and Alan Parker (Chapter 10) suggest, that this will be the role of 'other colleges' or the residual LEA sector for their respective clients. The emphasis is on service, on providing what the customer wants. I have reservations about the term 'access'. It implies that someone is let in to participate and the onus is on them to adapt: to learn the language of academic discourse, to adopt the culture of the institution, to accept its power structures, to change timetables and lifestyles to fit in, and to be assessed by it on its own undisclosed and unchallengeable criteria. I prefer concepts of openness and outreach. This last has long been a tradition in adult education: Hoggart (1990) describes his life as a peripatetic external lecturer, the equivalent of the boy-on-the-bike delivering your order to the doorstep.

Sheffield LEA pioneered work in drop-in centres in deprived parts of the city, though HMI (1986) had some difficulty coming to terms with the different criteria which operated. They regretted the loss of traditional AE (but the Workers' Educational Association (WEA) and university did that), were concerned about staff appointments where acceptability in the community ranked with academic qualifications, and had to adopt 'notional student numbers' as a concept, given irregular classes and lack of formal registers. That is an idea which some heads of department tried to get me to accept when I was an Academic Registrar and they were marginally below the minimum stipulated enrolment for a course. It requires a significant mind shift to embrace it. That is the point. If we are to reach out to those who need education and development, the onus is on *us* to change. It's no good having a polished product which nobody wants or which, after power selling, will be returned by a disillusioned customer. We must re-discover our communities and fit in with them. We should also recognize that much is going on quietly and unobtrusively in those communities to help develop citizens, through voluntary organizations, associations, clubs and self-help activities. Since building capacity is limited, open learning approaches may well increasingly be located in community settings anyway. Part-time and distance students preserve their community identities and networks and these, too, colleges need to recognize, as do their student unions. Older, 'occasional' students are not a captive market for societies, clubs, or committees.

Openness is not easy; it's not cheap; and it is very fragile. Commitment must be shared by all staff. It is no use having a policy of openness and equality if management will not fund access ramps or building alterations for those in wheelchairs; if a lecturer is arrogant and dismissive of students' life experiences; if a receptionist is fierce in the 'welcome' offered to those making a first tentative approach; if a caretaker makes racist jokes; if an over-zealous administrator insists that buildings close promptly at 9 p.m., or if support services are inadequate. Openness, like quality, has to be total. And, if we want post-compulsory education to avoid being just more of the same but adaptive to the new needs of the next century, for people who haven't yet been touched by it, the commitment to openness and quality also has to be total, at all levels, from government, to governors of colleges, to 'gofers'.

12

Quality: The Search for Quality

Judith Bell

Quality is in fashion. It is rarely possible to read educational journals, or even daily newspapers without coming across articles about quality. What is it? How do we know it is there? Why isn't there enough of it in our schools, colleges, polytechnics and universities? Statements from Ministers leave no doubt that we are short-changing our pupils and students and that academic standards are falling.

The prison service and the legal system, the police, civil service and local government have all come under fire, and the quality of service they provide questioned. So far, the quality of service provided by politicians has not been questioned in public, but perhaps their turn will come. We may even live to see the day when performance indicators are produced to measure the effectiveness of a Prime Minister, a Secretary of State for Education and Science or a Chancellor of the Exchequer. Perhaps the entries in *Who's Who* might then read 'Mr/Mrs/Ms x, Prime Minister/Secretary of State 19xx–19yy. Graded C on the quality measure.'

For all I know, politicians may regularly undergo analysis of their performance and the rigorous examination of their working practices before they get a salary increase. They may appoint Audit Commissions to examine their quality assurance and quality control mechanisms, to record levels of competence and to investigate staff development programmes for newly elected MPs. Perhaps they have peer review sessions in cabinet meetings. I wonder whether they have Key Stages (no Member of Parliament can be considered for a cabinet position unless he/she has reached Key Stage 5)? Perhaps all this happens. I have never mixed in sufficiently elevated society to know. I hope it does, because in spite of this flippant approach, it seems to me essential for each individual, each group, each organization not only to claim to provide a quality service, but to be able to demonstrate to outsiders how such claims can be substantiated. Government is no exception – but then, nor are schools, colleges, polytechnics or universities.

Some of the statements about falling standards give the clear impression that there has never been any quality assurance in this country. That is certainly not so. All the committed teachers and education managers I have known have as a matter of course looked back at their work and come to conclusions about the effectiveness of their teaching, their budgeting, their assessment procedures and their students' overall learning experience. They may not have used the words now in common usage, but they did the job. Good teachers always wanted to do better and to provide the very best for their students. The difference was that their version of quality assurance was a private matter, limited to the conscience of individuals or small groups. They did not make their methods public, *because no one ever asked them to do so.*

That approach worked perfectly well for the committed teachers and managers. The problem was of course that there was no check on those individuals who did not have the same commitment, skill and enthusiasm for the job.

Everything is not perfect in education. We all know that, though we may not admit it in public. Every organization has its dead wood (industry and government included), but the dead wood in education can have a devastating effect on the students who are unfortunate enough to be in their care. There are very few, but the effect they have on the rest can be serious. They are the ones who do the minimum amount of work, who never take their share of the disagreeable or difficult jobs, who have no sense of commitment to the students. They are the ones whose classes start late and finish early, who mark written work hastily and unhelpfully, who are never available to see students and who do not feel that time needs to be spent on preparation. They are there, and we know they are there, so why haven't we done anything about it? Just try proving it, if there has never been any attempt at quality assurance or quality control. We may 'know' they are doing a poor job but there is generally no hard evidence.

I appear to be concentrating on what is the worst of the profession and this may already be causing irritation to some readers. My years as one of Her Majesty's Inspectors left me in no doubt that the vast majority of teachers and education managers are committed, skilled and overworked. The point of my argument is that there is a tendency for the sins of the few to overshadow the virtues of the many. Ministers have been quick to point to the deficiencies of the education system and individual examples of such deficiencies are not hard to find. 'One of my constituents told me', or 'the other day I was talking to a parent who . . .' It is all too easy to cast doubts on the quality of the entire teaching profession by reference to individual cases.

In only a few cases have serious efforts been made systematically to judge the quality of the education we provide – and that comes down to the quality of teaching and managing. Until now. And now, all educational institutions are being compelled to address the problem of quality. Central government directives, many linked to finance, have forced us all to do what we should have done ourselves years ago. We have always balked at making judgements about colleagues or even about ourselves and we have comforted ourselves by saying 'it's not my business', 'it would be a gross infringement of personal liberties', 'teachers must at all costs retain their autonomy', 'it can't be done anyway' and 'there's nobody here capable of making judgements about my teaching'. I have heard them all.

The question of who would do the judging is frequently raised in connection with appraisal systems and much the same difficulties are presented as reasons why teachers serving their probationary period are sometimes left alone and then assumed to have been satisfactory.

Unbelievably, I have been through seven probationary periods in my time; two in English universities, two in colleges of FE, two in the DES and one in an American university. In six cases, I had a congratulatory letter at the end of the first year notifying me that I had successfully completed the probationary period and was now permanent/established/tenured. The Americans were different.

Only at the University of Wisconsin did anyone see my work at first hand. Wisconsin was an eye opener. I went there after I had been teaching for seven years. I was experienced, quite well qualified, fluent in Spanish and, I considered, hard working. At Wisconsin, they were not very impressed about that. It was no more than expected. Some people were better qualified, bilingual in more than one language and equally, if not more, hard working. I was required to attend a semester-long course on techniques of teaching Spanish. All newly appointed tutors were, no matter how experienced or well qualified.

My teaching was observed on eight occasions during my first year at Wisconsin and after each visit, I was interviewed and points of teaching style were discussed. I did not like those unannounced visits, any more than I imagine teachers in this country welcome visits from HMI, but during that year I learnt more about teaching than I had in the previous seven. Student feedback at the end of each course was automatic and an accepted part of the process. Our abilities, strengths and weaknesses were known and documented. If weaknesses were identified, efforts were made to help us to improve. If we did not improve, we were not reappointed. Tenure really meant something and it was not given under five years at the least.

It is 25 years since I left Wisconsin. Everything was not perfect then and I did not stay long enough to have to face the publications-for-tenure horror. It may be that 25 years has served to make me remember only the good parts and to eliminate the bad from my memory, but what remains with me is the recollection that I started teaching there with what I now see as a degree of complacence and that complacence was challenged. The Department of Spanish and Portuguese in those days aimed to provide a quality service for students and they attempted to provide what now would be called quality assurance and quality control systems. The emphasis was on providing the best possible service *for students*.

I have to confess the regime was ruthless. Only those who came up to standard survived but there is no doubt that the very small number of teachers who come into the 'dead wood' category in our institutions and who so discredit the profession, would have been removed at an early stage and that has to be good.

Looking back, I think there were several reasons why that rigorous regime was accepted by staff. Procedures for quality control were automatic. No one was exempt and everyone knew that. The unannounced visits provoked anxiety but they too were normal practice. Moreover, there was no doubt that the observers were themselves outstanding teachers. They knew what it was all about and were able to talk openly about their own practice. Student feedback was just one strand in a much wider scheme of appraisal and evaluation.

I have no doubt readers will have plenty of examples of American universities where there was no quality control and I have certainly come across examples of good practice in British colleges, polytechnics and universities. All I can say is that I have never come across any which took quite such care to ensure that the students came first and were not disadvantaged by having to suffer from poor teaching.

A great deal has been done in the last few years to raise the quality issue and to establish structures for monitoring performance. My great regret is that the impetus has tended to come from outside. Central government directives have forced institutions to consider appraisal, to introduce formal monitoring and evaluation procedures and to identify ways in which judgements can be made about quality.

For many years, we were never really asked to account for ourselves. As long as examination results and student attendance were reasonable, few questions were asked. Things could not go on like that and the government has made it clear that education has to toe the line.

One way in which institutions were encouraged or forced to change was through special funding. The MSC New Training Initiative began the debate in 1981, though concern about standards had been on the agenda long before then. This was followed by pronouncements, directives and earmarked funding, all of which were designed to obtain a greater degree of accountability from education and better value for the money being spent.

1985 saw the publication of *Obtaining Better Value from Further Education* which proposed basic measures of efficiency and which raised furious opposition in some quarters. From then on, discussion documents, reports and statements have proliferated and proposed measures of efficiency and effectiveness have become more sophisticated.

The Joint Efficiency Study, *Managing Colleges Efficiently*, published in 1987 made far-reaching recommendations on how to improve the management of resources in colleges and the message was reinforced by the FE Staff College publication *Managing Resources in Further Education* (D. Birch, 1988), published in the following year.

Then everyone joined in. The NAB, the UGC and its successor the UFC, the PCFC, the MSC, and its successors the Training Commission (TC) and the TA, the Committee of Vice Chancellors and Principals, the Committee of

Polytechnic Directors, the FEU and the validating bodies all produced their statements and discussion documents.

The Education Reform Act of 1988 made earlier recommendations into legal requirements and the government's intentions were made absolutely clear. Institutions of FE and HE were to be given greater financial autonomy to manage their own affairs but at the same time they were required to demonstrate the extent to which they were efficient and effective.

Since then, there has been an explosion in 'How to' publications relating to performance indicators, quality assurance and quality control systems, educational audits, budgetary control mechanisms and ways of ensuring quality in relation to specific aspects of teaching and learning. Quality in Open Learning, Quality in PICKUP, Quality in Non-advanced Further Education, Quality in Continuing Education. The MSC/TC/TA publications tend to be more glossy (some even with free pens attached to the cover), but whether high-cost productions or quickly produced handouts, the message is the same. We must get into line. We must learn how to account for ourselves and our finance. We must demonstrate how we are providing value for money. We must do better.

Models abound, including those devised for manufacturing industries. In the search for a solution to the problems of managing the new-style accountable institutions, some colleges have turned to service and manufacturing industry models and in particular BS5750 Total Quality Control. BS5750 is concerned with management procedures designed to ensure that a product (or service) is being produced consistently to its specifications. It is not directly concerned with quality but with procedures, which are checked by the British Standards Institution. The FEU is in the process of investigating quality assurance models planned or in place in colleges and the results of that investigation will be invaluable. The FEU makes the point that the ultimate test might well be whether any of the models in operation improves the quality of teaching and learning (FEU, 1990). That is what we need to know. Are manufacturing and other models right for education. Will they be sufficiently flexible for our purposes?

Much of the above relates to further education but higher education has certainly not been exempt from the government's campaign for better value for money. Universities, polytechnics, colleges and institutes of higher education have faced similar dilemmas. Threats of redundancy, closure of uneconomic departments and threats to tenure began to be heard.

The University Departments of Extra Mural Studies, some of which were classified as 'responsible bodies' and funded directly by the DES, came particularly under fire. The WEA which came under the same funding regulations was equally affected.

New funding regulations were introduced which linked funding to 'effective student hours'. If students were not 'effective' (that is, if they did not attend a stipulated minimum number of hours), the departments and the WEA districts did not receive funding for them.

This arrangement caused immense problems. The financial control systems of the departments and districts were not geared to such detailed head counting. They had never been asked to be accountable – at least, not in ways the DES was then demanding. For some time, in spite of the clear messages that were emerging from the DES, not all departments and districts accepted that the DES meant business. The belief was that the DES would never dare to interfere with the universities and they would get short shrift if they tried to disband the WEA. It was believed that there were too many MPs, including the leader of the opposition, who had at some time been involved with the WEA, either as students or tutors.

They were all wrong. The DES wanted evidence of what they did, how much it cost and whether it was worth spending money on. I was involved in many inspections of Departments of Extra Mural Studies and WEA district and branch programmes and I know most of the work was worth saving. Some of the work was inspiring. Committed tutors and committed students worked together to produce work of the highest quality, but as in other sectors, it was not all good and in very few cases had serious efforts been made to find out what was good and what was not of an acceptable standard. Heads of department 'knew' where the strengths and weaknesses of their departments lay and they were generally right, but when they came under attack from the DES, they were poorly placed to defend themselves by producing evidence of the quality and cost effectiveness of their provision.

They had never been asked to do that and there were, after all, many other more pressing matters to deal with. Now, they too must toe the line, but they are faced with more severe problems than institutions which have a predominantly full-time student body. Most of the guidelines directed at further and higher education are difficult to relate to adult and continuing education.

The FEU Bulletin of June 1990, *Performance Indicators in the Education and Training of Adults* draws attention to the problems of transferability of models designed with full-time students in mind. Adult education institutions are faced with the problems of managing courses and programmes of varying length. Students generally attend on a discontinuous basis and AE and continuing education services do their best to provide for what the Russell Report described as the 'life-long but discontinuous needs' to 'correspond with the unpredictable development of people's abilities and aspirations at all ages'.

Crude measures of efficiency are not likely to be sufficient to take account of the variation in mode, content and timing of continuing education activities.

The Unit for the Development of Adult Continuing Education (UDACE) and several LEAs and colleges have already begun work on devising indicators and assessment techniques for judging the effectiveness of education for adults (UDACE, 1990) and more will need to be done to ensure in particular that non-vocational adult education is not swept along the performance indicator route without due consideration being given to the particular circumstances in which programmes for adults are provided.

The same caution must be exacted in relation to all parts of the education system, of course. This point has been well made by Professor P.A. Reynolds, formerly Vice Chancellor of the University of Lancaster and chairman of the CVCP group on academic standards. In the foreword to the 1986 CVCP paper on academic standards in universities (Reynolds, 1986), he wrote:

> Quality has no meaning except in relation to purpose or function. A car that is of high quality for racing purposes would not be of high quality for comfortable travelling and vice versa. The quality of a higher education system can be evaluated only in terms of the extent to which it achieves the purpose for which the system is intended . . . For a Secretary of State, a high quality system might be one that produces sufficient trained scientists and engineers, for an industrialist it might be one that turns out graduates with flexible and adaptable minds, for an academic it might be one that provides a steady flow of scholars. Clarity and consistency require that references to 'maintaining' or 'improving' the quality of higher education should always be placed in the context of the purposes to which the speaker or writer gives priority.

This makes perfect sense to me. The context must, necessarily, have a direct influence on the type of measures used. That is why I am so fearful of externally imposed performance indicators being imposed to conform to some sort of national model. And even if the government had not demanded proof of value for money, no institution can afford not to look critically at its own structures and the quality of service provided for its students.

The Lindop Report (1985, paragraph 7.4) made the valid point that 'the most reliable safeguard of standards is not external validation or any other outside control; it is the growth of the teaching institution as a self-critical community'. If that self-criticism is absent, then the institution will inevitably stagnate.

Reynolds (1986) made a similar point when he stated that 'no society is healthy that is not subject to a sustained and informed critique of its structure and of behaviour in it', and 'the constant advance of knowledge requires constant reconsideration of the procedures that are appropriate for the maintenance of quality and standards'.

The problem we have all faced in recent years is proving that we carry out these procedures – that we are self-critical and do reconsider procedures that are appropriate for the maintenance of quality and standards in our particular context. It goes without saying that a further problem lies in the fact that no one is likely to disagree with Lindop and Reynolds, but if the structures for putting policy into practice are not in place, nothing will happen.

In an interview with Rosalind Yarde for the *Times Higher Educational Supplement* on 6 July 1990, Peter Williams, the head of the recently established Universities Academic Audit Unit said that, 'Universities maintain that they produce quality products. But it always struck me that they opened themselves to criticism if anyone said "prove it".' He stressed that the Unit was not being established because of concern that standards were falling but of 'a need for universities to show and explain to the world at large what they are doing'. He was concerned to ensure 'that the universities don't disadvantage themselves by ignoring the question'. I hope so too.

There can never be one set of rules, one model, to cover all circumstances, but if we do not try to identify our own particular circumstances and ways of determining quality *in our own context*, then the danger is that some outsider who holds the purse strings is likely to impose a blanket requirement which will be inappropriate for everyone. If we do not have our alternatives ready, we shall have no right to complain.

13

Technology: Technological Utopias in Post-compulsory Education

David Hawkridge

More than 100 years ago, my grandfather had in mind a technological Utopia in education. He read science at Cambridge and became the first Superintendent for Technical Education in Derbyshire. His papers and speeches about the need for technical education at England's industrial heart attracted some attention. Regrettably, he died in 1897 at the age of 34.

He was ahead of his time. British education has a Luddite past. In my grandfather's day, science and technology were not much respected in educational circles. Education was a bookish system, modelled on ecclesiastical traditions at the ancient universities. Despite the Industrial Revolution, academics took a long time to move away from their scholarly study of text – some still do not. Many eminent colleges had no science laboratories or workshops until well into the twentieth century. Teacher trainers paid very little attention to science and looked down on the technical subjects as 'handcraft'. Even distinguished educationists like Alfred North Whitehead (1932) held a limited 'liberal arts' view of science and technology in the curriculum.

After the Second World War and then Sputnik, science and technology entered education like a rush of blood to the head. The curriculum changed fast because science acquired new status, with technology close behind. Scientists and engineers were at last respected: without them we might never have won the war. There were structural changes too. Colleges of Advanced Technology grew into fully fledged universities. Polytechnics were founded, with a utilitarian and technological orientation. Investment in laboratories, workshops and other appropriate buildings rocketed. Student numbers rose, though not as quickly as expected. Were school-leavers sceptical about technological Utopias?

The teaching of science and technology became much more scientific. Professors and lecturers in science departments believed that the best way to learn about science was by doing it. Twenty-five years ago, their Utopia was an excellently equipped laboratory. The engineers became more science- and workshop-oriented, too. Bright students were to learn to be true scientists or technologists, like their professors.

In the 1960s, there was substantial interest in universities and colleges in using new technology to aid the teaching of science and technology. Any technological teaching medium of help in bringing about this Utopia was welcomed, from 16 mm film to tape-recordings. Any teaching method that claimed to embody scientific principles aroused some attention, even programmed learning. Description and discussion of experiments in using these methods filled new periodicals devoted to advancing the teaching of different disciplines, as well as demanding space in older research-oriented journals. The Open University was started against this exciting background, and many of its original teaching staff were keen to apply the 'educational sciences' to distance education at the post-compulsory level. The university became famous for, amongst other things, its novel and extensive use of technological media in undergraduate education.

Across the Atlantic, influenced by the need to keep up-to-date in the Cold War, government-funded bodies poured people and money into research and development programmes. Among these were some aimed at deploying computers for teaching, as fast as possible throughout HE. Even in the days of clumsy mainframes, many North American academics were convinced that undergraduates had to be educated better by using them, not merely for teaching computer science. Dartmouth College led the way, not least in developing the computer language BASIC. The Pierce (1967) Report, from a panel of the US President's Science Advisory Committee, came up with 10 recommendations, including the Utopian proposal that all university and college students should have access to computing facilities. To follow this up, the National Science Foundation set up an Office of Computing Activities, which promoted and funded over the next decade large numbers of projects aimed at using mainframe computers for teaching in US post-compulsory education. Each year, starting in 1970, a huge conference heard reports on these and other similar projects. The titles of the papers from the first one reveal an astonishing range, from computer-animated film for art at Ohio State University, to computers in engineering design, to computer games to teach macroeconomics and simulation models in oceanography. To judge from the authors' enthusiastic but uncritical approach, they were technological Utopians.

Lack of money, machines and conviction meant that British developments were slower and smaller, perhaps with less effort wasted on dead-ends. When I arrived at the Open University from the USA in January 1970, the DES was not yet convinced that the Open University needed a computer, even for administrative purposes. It took a year or so for us to get our own computer on which to register our first 43,000 applicants. Computers for teaching and research purposes took a little longer, and we were lucky compared with many other British post-compulsory education institutions at that time. The National Development Programme in Computer-Assisted Learning (see Hooper and Toye, 1975; Hooper, 1977) gave computers a lingering glance, with few results. Harold Wilson's 'white-hot technological revolution' turned some things over rather slowly.

I was surprised when a Labour government, under James Callaghan, perceived the urgent need to move faster towards a technological Utopia. Some say it was the television programme (a technological teaching medium), 'The Chips are Down', that convinced the Cabinet. By the time Margaret Thatcher moved into 10 Downing Street, other leaders in Europe were interested. For once, the British took action while others were still being rhetorical. In 1980, Christian Beullac, the French Minister of Education, spoke of 'le mariage du siècle', the wedding of information technology to education, yet French efforts to use computers widely in their schools and colleges lag behind the British.

Early in the 1980s, microcomputers arrived. They rapidly became ubiquitous. Not that mainframes were pushed out entirely; instead, computing power was distributed much more widely. Many teachers began to realize how microcomputers could help them, and that they were accessible, not locked away in distant rooms guarded by technicians.

By the mid-1980s, academics in every discipline were being persuaded by colleagues that word-processing with microcomputers was by far the best way of preparing books, papers, lecture notes, journal articles, book reviews and all the other sorts of creative and original compilations that made up their written output. The secretaries might still be working on typewriters, but research proposals now often included requests for money to purchase microcomputers, for use of academics, despite the occasional trade union concern over potential secretarial job losses. Computer scientists and mathematicians were a little slower than the rest of us, being wedded to the notion that computers were for worthier purposes.

Perhaps surprisingly, in view of the interest in using mainframe computers in undergraduate education, British post-compulsory institutions were quite slow to introduce microcomputers into their teaching. The late 1980s brought networks, students with microcomputers of their own, and new forms of storage and delivery, such as the videodisc and compact disk ('disc' derived from 'gramophone disc', and 'disk' from computer 'diskette').

British universities received a shot in the arm when the Government agreed in 1986 to put several millions into the Computers in Teaching Initiative (CTI), with three aims: to encourage development of computer-assisted teaching and learning; to evaluate the educational potential of information technology; and to promote awareness of this potential among lecturers and students in all disciplines. The work has spread to polytechnics.

Institutions responded, quite slowly, as their teaching staff tried to come to terms with the new technology and as resources were diverted to purchasing the hardware and software. In the first phase, up to 1988, there were 139 courseware development projects under CTI's auspices. Between them, they produced a large quantity of software and course materials. In the second phase, 21 CTI Centres were set up in 1989, all coordinated and assisted by the CTI Support Service, based in Oxford University. These subject-based centres promote and evaluate the use of computers in teaching their disciplines. Individually, they have conducted surveys of what is happening and what is needed. They maintain computerized databases on software. They circulate newsletters and software reviews. An electronic bulletin board operates through the JANET academic network: over 3000 screens of information have gone out so far. By May 1990, 18 conferences and 45 workshops had been held or planned. Together, the Centres are assessing hardware, software and organizational issues in using computers more widely in university teaching.

What is the flavour of the CTI's products? Just one issue of *The CTISS File*, No. 7, for October 1988, contains reports on work in medical education, dietetics, archaeology, civil engineering, biological sciences, chemistry, physics, geography, history, art education and design, foreign languages, information studies, classical languages, business management, mathematics and political science. Some authors are enthusiastic, even Utopian in their outlook, but most are sober appraisals, containing frank discussion of problems. A political science lecturer from the London School of Economics dwells on the need to avoid the trap of too much interactivity, too little analysis in dealing with a text-based discipline such as his own. In contrast, two lecturers in German from King's College, London, explain why they felt a computerized database of 'German for special purposes' was valuable in their teaching, making it more learner-specific. A lecturer in history at Southampton University describes how a research project in historical demography in Portugal led to the development of a very large teaching database, held on the University's large computer but downloaded as needed to microcomputers for student use. None of these examples is in the so-called scientific disciplines, in which computers seem to lay-people to have many more uses.

An evaluation of the CTI in 1989 reported that at least 25,000 students a year are using CTI-originated software. Up to then, over 800 staff had become directly associated with the initiative.

At my own university, where students of computer science in the 1970s had access to mainframes through teletype terminals in study centres, a revolution occurred as academics and computer support staff realized that microcomputers would change the approach needed. After agonizing over dangers such as speedy obsolescence, Senate adopted the MS-DOS (MicroSoft's Disk Operating System) software standard instead of the more up-to-date Unix, and authorized obligatory use of microcomputers on several courses. In 1990, over 13,000 students were taking these, about a sixth of the total enrolment on all undergraduate courses. The numbers were projected to rise to 17,300 by 1992. At the Open University, we do not see a technological Utopia before us, but we are constantly trying to find new ways to exploit the latest developments, in the interests of our students. We have led the field in computer conferencing, for example, which links students and students, students and tutors. If a cheap flat-screen device appears that enables us to send our students parts of their courses on magnetic disk in digital form, we shall probably experiment with it, as we did with video-cassettes, videodiscs and other electronic media.

Meantime, from the early 1980s microcomputers invaded campuses in the USA in very large numbers. A milestone was passed when Carnegie-Mellon University in Pittsburgh decreed that every student admitted should have his or her own microcomputer. Other campuses felt obliged to follow suit. The National Science Foundation financed software exchanges, to increase use of campus-made programmes. Each item had to be thoroughly tested before acceptance. Prices were subsidized. Computer companies fostered development and exchange. Other less formally organized exchanges sprang into being, and pirating or free exchange became common. With such universal access to computing power came the 'tool' software for students to use: word-processing, graphics and statistical packages, spreadsheets and data-bases. Students who ignored these were simply depriving themselves of a golden opportunity to learn skills likely to be of value throughout their professional and private lives.

All these developments have cost a great deal, and there has been no lack of critics, who have said that resources should have gone elsewhere, that technological Utopias are not only unattainable but undesirable. So, in the nineties, shall we see more rapid movement towards these Utopias in post-compulsory education? My own view is that we shall. Behind computers and communications technology are extremely powerful political and economic forces. It is not merely a question of large international companies wanting to make greater profits, though they are undoubtedly a factor. Governments of industrialized nations – and even some developing ones – have convinced themselves, if not their constituencies, that information technology is essential in the economic race. National well-being may be at stake. It is inconceivable that this creative gale of destruction will miss post-compulsory education. The old methods will be in part destroyed and new technologically based ones will take their place.

We all know teachers in our institutions who still live in ivory towers and show their ignorance as they blandly assert that microcomputers are playthings in the classroom, and word-processors merely expensive typewriters. They have failed to grasp the significance of the information technology revolution. In priding themselves on defending old teaching traditions, they may well be clinging to personal power. One colleague of mine used to speak grandly of how he 'taught *ex cathedra*', with all the wisdom and experience of his 29 years, and 'set high standards' – by failing the majority of his class. Technology gives short shrift to such arrogance, because it can open the books of knowledge, giving students access to what was formerly a privilege of the few. Many teachers are keen to use the technology for themselves and to see their students using it, as the CTI has shown. Potentially, information technology can have a significant impact on curriculum and methods. Consider the libraries: every library in post-compulsory education is moving towards full computerization of its search facilities, and students are coming to expect as much. Consider the teachers, whose role is changing as students become more independent as learners, drawing for themselves on computer-ized 'knowledge banks'. Given that less classroom contact time is required, teachers can increase their teaching and research productivity through using the technology. Some may tutor students through electronic mail or computer conferencing, and some may link up electronically with foreign researchers in their field. Others may exploit the international computerized databases, which can somewhat compensate for the rapid obsolescence of print-based knowledge.

Student numbers are set to increase, without the money to build more classrooms or even to refurbish old buildings. There is a demographic decline of the age-group from which the lecturers are drawn. Change is likely to occur faster and faster over the next decade as institutions adapt to such circumstances. Part of that change will be through bringing more technology into education, to increase effectiveness and efficiency.

Effective use of this technology in AD 2000 will depend on good manage-ment. Its Utopian potential will only be realized if managers can provide the right conditions for teachers and learners to exploit the machines rather than be exploited by them. If large amounts of money were diverted to IT from, say, libraries or some other valuable aspect of education, then teachers and learners could justifiably claim they were being exploited. The debate on such questions of value will be a continuing one, in which managers must expect to participate.

Managers keen to exploit the technology will have to overcome the prob-lems of hardware obsolescence, which already trouble many post-compulsory educational institutions. It is not so much a case of the hardware wearing out quickly: most information technology no longer requires kid gloves and air-conditioning. Rather, obsolescence occurs because more powerful and faster hardware is being developed very quickly indeed. Engineering students need to gain experience of very modern automated equipment instead of being condemned to old-fashioned workshop practice, medical students need to use equipment for laser surgery as well as knowing how to dissect, music students need to explore the latest electronic methods of composition, sociol-ogy students need to learn the latest statistical packages. All of these usually require the latest hardware. New versions of software will not run on old hardware.

Managers will also have to find or commission culturally suitable educa-tional software. I mention cultural suitability because software is transferred to other countries with as much difficulty as textbooks – and we all know how few foreign textbooks are used in post-compulsory education in this country. It goes without saying that the software must run on the hardware, much of it imported from the Far East or the USA, but the software must also be acceptable within British courses. Even in mathematics courses this can be a problem because of different notation.

Finally, managers will have to meet the fierce criticisms of some academics who, like Canute's courtiers, want to stop what they perceive as an advanc-ing tide of merchants of knowledge. For example, there are the followers of

Lyotard (1984), whose message about the 'post-modern condition of know-ledge' in present-day Western industrialized society is that capitalists are turning knowledge into a commodity, to be bought and sold in a marketplace which they dominate. Lyotard rails against such a political fate for our culture. One disciple, Fox (1989), even sees open and distance learning – perhaps an up-and-coming technological Utopia – as a branch of the 'know-ledge industry'. He asserts, somewhat grandly, that the nature, production and distribution of knowledge is changing under their impact (and the impact of IT), and compares this shift to that of the Renaissance, when personal speculation replaced divine revelation. Humanism undermined the divine. Now technology is undermining the human. He is very concerned about the iron entering the soul. Politically, he says, knowledge is now being used to give power to a new international class of decision-makers in govern-ment, industry and business. More and more, 'knowledge and the opportun-ity to learn are benefits to be bought by private individuals rather than fundamental rights belonging to every member of a democracy'. Open and distance learning become a 'dream instrument' for the control of the ruled, he avers (to the surprise of those of us engaged in designing this learning).

Managers, by their nature, are in a weak position to rebuff such criticism. They are suspect just because they are managers – from vice-chancellors downwards, of course. In these days of rampant market-forces it seems very likely indeed to the underdogs that the merchants of knowledge will enter into vastly profitable alliances with the managers. If it happens, this will simply confirm what the underdogs knew all along, that they can never win. Utopias are only for bosses, aren't they?

14

Structure: Restructuring and Resourcing

Ian McNay

Significant shifts

If the shifts in patterns of participation (see Chapter 11) have not been as great as those committed to a radical view of access would have wished, and seem likely to continue to disappoint them, there *have* been radical shifts in the patterns of organization, control and funding of post-compulsory education and training. The trends will probably continue to consolidate and extend what has already happened. Chapter 3 gives a view of the de-structuring within an institution, and Chapter 15 outlines a more deliberate attempt to relocate management functions in modified structures for planning and control.

This chapter attempts to link curriculum with resource and postulates three main trends, each with several strands. The first is the shift from input to output; the second counters Schuller's fission with evidence of fusion; the third examines the emergence of new levels of operational and policy significance: activity/cost centres within institutions and the gradual displacement of a local/national system with one with more regional/international dimensions.

Input to output: The three customers

For many years, investment in education was an act of faith. Human capital theory linked economic and social development to levels of education in the population. Teachers at all levels were held in esteem and assumed to teach to the benefit of their students. Individuals deferring gratification and sacrificing several years of income to continue their study believed this would be of long-term benefit, in better jobs, including higher income. All these have come under challenge. There have been recurrent economic crises and a slow decline in Britain's position in the world economic league. Employers have criticized education as irrelevant, of low standard in ensuring a work-force with basic skills and as promoting anti-industrial, anti-capitalist attitudes. The gap between graduate salaries and the average wage has narrowed – ironically the most graphic representation of this was in the White Paper introducing student loans (DES, 1989d). Part of the explanation lies in the increase in graduates in public sector service posts, where traditionally pay has been lower. In future, there may well be 'welcome bonuses' offered by employers to retain recruitment levels from the smaller cohorts of school leavers, especially those whose decision to continue in full-time education is finely balanced.

The result has been to give more emphasis to 'the customer' in tune with the ascendancy of free-market ideas. But this doesn't mean that the role of the state has reduced: the state is customer as well as sponsor. Neave (1988) plots the emergence across Europe of the 'evaluative state'. In the UK this was encapsulated in Sir Keith Joseph's Green Paper (DES, 1986) which, while accepting 'ability to benefit' as the criterion for entry to HE stipulated that the benefit had to be such as to justify the cost. As the state bore the cost, it should also judge the benefit. So, the 1991 White Paper (HMSO, 1991c) avers that 'student demand should not be the sole determinant of the shape of expansion ... an element of institutional grant ... will allow the development of higher education to be steered, *as required* (with) funding ... linked with assessments of quality' (emphasis added). The state, therefore, commissions products from institutions, via the intermediary councils, somewhat as Marks & Spencer does from its suppliers, with a similar control because of its near-monopoly dominance of their 'business'.

Judith Bell deals with quality definition and measurement in Chapter 12. It is worth noting here, however, that whereas the UGC used entry qualifications as a major indicator of quality, the emphasis has shifted to outcomes. The CVCP points to the increase in graduates with first-class honours degrees; the CDP emphasizes 'education value added' since their staff are more adept at turning apparently base metal into gold – or at least letting the shining qualities of students without traditional entry qualifications emerge from the veneer of dullness with which others had painted them.

The power of this second customer – the learner – is also being enhanced. The chapter on outreach and openness recorded some examples of the greater attention now being paid to researching and responding to their needs. The next ten years may well see formal 'learning contracts' and customer 'charters' with more attention to learner needs and customer care by institutions to avoid claims for compensation when they fall short of acceptable standards: if British Rail pays compensation when trains are late, should the same apply to lecturers? The shift of emphasis from teaching to learning is, in my view, the most important long-term development for the health of post-compulsory education and those it serves. Fuller statements of what can be expected by participation, a rigorous scrutiny of the quality of design and delivery of programmes – including support services – and a fuller understanding of the transformation processes involved in learning are long overdue. Learning also unites the academic community in a single common goal: it resolves the teaching/research dichotomy if research is seen as 'discovery learning' and teaching/supervision/project leadership as promoting learning at different levels. It pushes teachers and trainers to be learners too when many have seemed to be static in their own development, and creates a more equal partnership with others which helps the transmission and transformation processes. And if all staff have a common purpose of supporting student learning, 'support staff' becomes a positive label to replace the hierarchical 'non-teaching', 'non-academic' negative classifications used hitherto.

The UDACE project on learning outcomes is one contribution to this debate, pushing academics to reflect on the consequences of their activities and encouraging students and employers to be clearer about their expectations. At the time of writing the last group are again being exposed as having not worked through the issue of what a graduate should be, should be able to do and how they would use them which other reports had already indicated (Cassels, 1990; HMSO, 1990). The students gave more emphasis to personal and social objectives than to vocational ones (Thorne, 1991). Staff views varied by discipline area with, for example, English lecturers giving prominence to critical thinking but not creativity and engineers doing the opposite (UDACE, 1991).

That project recognizes, too, the shift from *acquisition* of learning to its *application* and here representatives of employers – which the Scottish White Paper of 1991 (HMSO, 1991a) recognized as the 'ultimate consumers' of vocational education – have been active. Many Lead Industry Bodies did, though, adopt, initially, a narrow, task-centred approach to the definition of competences at lower NVQ levels. The 1991 White Papers moved away from this to *general* NVQs, a welcome liberalization which allayed some fears among educators and is essential if NVQs are to gain credence at higher levels. The Enterprise in Higher Education project has assisted this in attempts to define, assess and grade 'core' competences.

There has been some integration, too, of the applied experience into the academic domain. For many years there was little or no assessment even of work on placement in sandwich courses – it existed almost apart from the course of which it was a part, at least in operative structure if not in curriculum design. Now, with the development of credit transfer there is the emergence of credit by assessment of experiential learning *not* designed and planned specifically for such a purpose – though the high staff time needed for bespoke assessment may mean expansion of this will be slow. Significantly, some of this learning was achieved without a 'teacher'. In the last few years of its existence the CNAA also recognized centres based on organizations where education/training was a supportive ancillary activity to their main purpose. HMI even conducted inspections of Sainsbury's YTS training. So the training given to an assistant manager of a burger-bar can count for credit within a BTEC HND and a business studies degree. In the USA, corporations offer their own programmes to MSc and PhD level (Eurich, 1985) and as global communications improve, there is no reason why the international conglomerates should not make these available in learning centres in their branches world-wide.

This shift to work-based learning may be acceptable with the recognition of the need for constant thorough career updating, which can be seen as another shift – from pre-entry education to post-entry training and development. There is concern, though, that employers may screen selectively the material which learners use, or the interpretations put upon it. Just as distance learning is used by some countries to stop the concentration on campus of a critical mass of dissidents (Rumble, 1986), so over-emphasis on work-based learning, located in the workplace, is used to restrict the richer, more varied exchange of experience possible when staff are released to study with others. There may even be concerns about commercial confidentiality – which was why nineteenth-century science teaching in universities was confined to theory after representations from employers.

This recognition of the importance of learners and learning outside education institutions goes alongside constitutional and financial changes whereby those outside education now assume greater interest and learners more 'buying power' in those institutions. The 1988 Education Reform Act required employers to be the majority on governing bodies of the new polytechnic corporations, and on the funding councils for both sides of the, then, binary line. The 1991 White Papers planned to exclude LEAs from all representation in post-16 provision in colleges despite their role in providing a near-monopoly of feeder courses, and in democratically representing the electorate of the general community. They are excluded in favour of designated representatives of industry, commerce and the professions, and the TECs. The Labour Party aims to keep the Councils, and much other policy has been bi-partisan, especially over HE so continuity can be expected (see Chapter 10).

Increasingly, over the 1980s, education was seen as a tool of capitalism. The 1987 White Paper (DES, 1987a) saw the main function of HE as to 'serve the economy more effectively' and the 1991 series (HMSO, 1991a,b,c) aimed to provide what employers want but what employers will not provide. Their overall tone was that state funding would go to prospective employees not to citizens of the polity so that personal and social education were left as residual responsibilities of local authorities.

Much of the funding is increasingly specific and related to output objectives. General liberal adult education is out of favour – it should be cost recovery from fees as should what is labelled 'leisure provision'. That raises questions of definition: is an interest in Europe in 1993 and after necessarily or exclusively vocational? Is the study of the nineteenth-century novel obviously personal or could it show access capability for study in HE? The fate of the WEA and university extra-mural departments must depend on how far they can reach accommodation with, rather than suffer incorporation into, the emergent dominant instrumental paradigms of FE and HE. This reinforces Leni Oglesby's Europe-wide concerns (see Chapter 8).

Private funding of education is also increasingly via specific sponsorship and less from philanthropic general patronage. This parallels developments elsewhere and, as Paxman (1990) points out over arts sponsorship, there is need for a visible return (on output measure) on the sponsor's money so that it can be counted as advertising for tax purposes. The benefit is not only commercial, but curricular. A clear majority of sponsored chairs in Law in recent years has been in the field of commercial law (with others in European Law with commercial emphasis). Family law is one area not so blessed. Development is therefore imbalanced and in any period of financial stringency the existence of sponsorship could protect areas differentially and distort the overall curriculum, because that is what one set of 'customers' wants, and pays for.

There is strong potential for such curriculum shifts at system level – via state sponsorship. The power of the intermediary bodies has diminished: UFC and PCFC have been seen more as instruments of government policy than the UGC and even NAB; auguries for the new bodies are not good, and LEAs are being stripped of authority and assets. Schemes such as PICKUP, and initiatives in biotechnology and teacher shortage subjects could be seen as developmental and legitimate marginal adjustments to the totality of curriculum offerings. Now the potential for government control via finance permeates the system. This is still so, even where the power of the student consumer is ostensibly increased. Training credits are for those who leave school and take vocational courses, not those who stay to take A levels. Loans for higher education and the reduction in value of grants will push students to part-time study – which they must finance themselves or via an employer sponsor – or to a choice of course where sponsorship of full-time study is available.

It seems likely that the machinery for paying grants will, anyway, change. Local Authorities, hard pressed by tighter government controls over their general finance and the chaos of the poll tax, have delayed paying the fees element of grants to institutions. Since central government has shifted the balance of funding from block grant to student fees as part of 'empowering' the customer, they now form a substantial part of an institution's total budget, so the effect of these delays is significant. The likely response, implied by a silence in the 1991 White Papers – though there is specific reference to *discretionary* awards – is that *mandatory* grants will be centralized and 'privatized' by being administered by the company handling student loans.

The shifts then reinforce one another – away from the priesthood in the temples of learning to lay people who may be not even agnostic about what has developed over centuries but antagonistic to it. While I don't share the extent of David Morrell's gloom, I do share his concern to protect the good while promoting necessary change.

Coming together: integration, coordination, standardization

Before the collapse of registrations for mathematics (see Chapter 11) the biggest growth in A levels was among students of combinations which crossed the two cultures divide. One strength of the polytechnics was the development of courses that drew on several disciplines focused on problem-solving fields of application – systems analysis, surveying, the environment. The development of modular courses, despite its apparent fissiparous base, allowed students to develop new combinations of traditional disciplines in a personal synthesis. The Business Education Council and, after merger, BTEC, encouraged both modularity and synthesis by emphasizing 'themes' not subjects and by introducing cross-modular assignments using assessment as an integrating device. In FE, the old 'liberal studies' with its complementary or contrasting design bases moved to cross-college curriculum concerns – language and IT across the curriculum both featured in several FEU projects. The Research Councils recognized the criticism that real problems don't fit nicely with single-discipline approaches and solutions; and sponsored centres related to issues, not subjects and interdisciplinary higher degree schemes developed.

This recognition of epistemological continuity has affected organizational structures, with mergers, linkages and 'rationalization' as recurrent themes, though more remains to be done. Education and training are now increasingly seen as complementary and interdependent but competition between respective responsible ministries, at least in England, has stunted any growth of them together (see Chapter 9). A single ministry to cover both cannot be long away, though there may then be a new division with 'Science' going elsewhere – to Industry? The abolition of the binary line is in part a recognition that the commonalities of institutions are greater than their differences and parity of esteem might be better assured by a single funding operation.

There is concern, however, that the trend towards convergence will be reinforced, that unity will mean conformity not diversity. Certainly the Open University is worried about how far the new structures, which have bipartisan political support, will recognize its unique pattern of activity. It remains to be seen whether the trappings of equality – by title, by a common funding base (when it comes) as well as a common channel, and a single student recruitment clearing house – will allow polytechnics and colleges to relax and pursue a different set of missions. The concern of their directors over titles does not give confidence. Their claim that the term 'polytechnic' is not understood abroad raises questions about their knowledge of European polytechnics from Gdansk to Athens, the prestige of France's École Polytechnique and, further afield, the clone Polytechnic in Hong Kong. Several European countries – Finland and Czechoslovakia are two examples – are currently developing a binary system not dissimilar to the UK, post-1966. If national funding councils for FE do emerge, similar concerns will arise as to whether distinctive traditions can be maintained and built upon, or whether one will come to dominate. If further tertiary college structures emerge the record of the pioneers gives hope in terms of access, effectiveness and efficiency. In many of them, indeed, the concern is that there has not been more mixing of the cultures.

After the 1988 Education Reform Act, there were hopes that AE and FE could find common ground and learn from one another reflected in the merger of the FEU and the Unit for the Development of Adult and Continuing Education. The 1991 White Papers re-created a divide between the two.

It seems likely, however, that other distinctions will diminish or disappear. Full- and part-time students study already in the same classroom and an individual may pursue a qualification by a mix of modes and, therefore, elude classification. The distinction between initial and continuing education is also blurring when many 'mature' students are pursuing 'initial' qualifications, even on a full-time basis, after a break from study or in mid-career. Credit transfer will blur the identification of any unit of study with any prescribed qualification.

These trends have led to the emergence of new roles in institutions. The first is that of adviser/counsellor to help learners through a destructuring system. The second is that of coordinator who approaches the chaos from the other end in trying to create an organizational coherence drawing together common elements from previously discrete activities. Their problem is often that they are lower paid innovators negotiating with established powerful figures trying to retain their crumbling empires.

Strata shifts in power, policy and purse string control

What will tip the balance in their negotiation is the power of resource. The coordinators, or 'activity managers' (McNay, 1989a), are increasingly becoming managers also of cost centres as activities are costed for funding submissions, budgetary control and accountability. They may also be specifically resourced by targeted allocations of earmarked funds from funding bodies. By the end of the decade/century with the shifts in staff identity recorded by Schuller, they could well be operating on an internal market and be semi-privatized so that any 'permanent' staff who remain would offer their services in competition – in quality and price – with colleagues and, perhaps, outside staff accepting part-time contracts. Existing heads of department, then, will be concerned to develop quality staff to justify their higher price, and ensure that activity managers buy in from what they can offer.

If the level at which funds are allocated and accounted for is moving 'down', the level at which resources are sought and overall funding policy determined seems to be moving 'up' the levels of the system. One leading university registrar believes that by the end of the century most of the funding of post-school education will come from 'Europe'. Many of the initiatives in FE currently gain considerable support from the various social funds, more so in the UK than any other country in the EC (Brunskill, 1990). Much of this is linked to economic regeneration or to training both of which are legitimate EC interests under the Treaty of Rome. 'Education' as such has been seen as excluded from its provisions, but, as education is seen increasingly as vocational/professional, more and more mainstream activity can be seen as covered by 'the rules'. Compare what happened when the then MSC was given funding powers for work related FE: LEAs immediately saw most provision as 'work related'; A levels helped *get* a job even if they didn't help you *do* the job. Acronymic European initiatives – TEMPUS, ERASMUS, etc. – already have enough funding clout to justify regular trips to Brussels by academics, and, for FE and vocational training, the establishment by LEAs and colleges of permanent 'lobby' appointments.

This emergence of the European factor will have curriculum and structural consequences. The rapid growth in numbers studying languages at A and H levels is one manifestation, as is the pressure for A level reform to bring the rest of the UK more in line with Scotland and the European mainland. Eurobusiness and Eurolaw boom in higher education and the older universities are switching language courses to modern usage in context away from centuries old literature. As credit transfer and mutual recognition of qualifications gain prominence on the international stage from 1993 the impact will increase though, it is to be hoped, not in a little Europe way at the expense of third world studies (see Chapter 16) or world literature.

Much European funding reflects the greater emphasis on regional levels of government and the regions as the focus for economic development, and, equally, requires cooperation among consortia of educational institutions. This reinforces the need for regional structures in education. There are already successful 'top-down' precedents in the funding and support to PICKUP and Replan, and 'bottom-up' initiatives in credit transfer consortia, access validation groups, and joint courses. I have argued elsewhere (McNay, 1991) the case for fuller partnership at regional level in economic regeneration, research and development and staff training. What I wish to do to conclude this chapter is present the case – inevitable, but also desirable in terms of self-interest – for cooperation among education providers. In part it is to rediscover a collective identity, in part to promote quality and efficiency. This may be foreshadowed by the anticipated regional committees in the proposed new structure for funding and control of FE, and by the national regional funding councils for higher education:

1. *If* growth of provision is to include more and more mature students who are geographically restricted in choice, or indeed, *if* more school-leavers in HE are forced by reductions in grant to study part-time from a home base, they need to have a full curriculum choice. A single institution cannot offer everything especially in minority subjects; so, *if* part-time courses are better if linked to full-time versions, there needs to be cooperative curriculum planning (rationalization?) to ensure availability of accessible provision and continuity of study without excessive disruption. There

are a number of LEAs with only one FE college which cannot meet all needs, so students already cross boundaries.
2. When UGC and PCFC merge, *if* 150 institutions is too big a span of control for effective central direction, and *if* FE/HE links are to continue to be fostered *if*/when LEAs lose control of colleges to regional committees, a regional structure for an integrated post-compulsory provision is an obvious intermediate level in England as well as the nation regions.
3. *If* quality is to be a key issue, *if* research is one key to quality in HE, but must be concentrated in centres of excellence, and *if* exchange of good practice is a good form of staff development and institutional development, there needs to be provision for staff secondments and exchanges within a regional consortium which could also provide a structure for quality assessment of its members, and even form a 'quality circle'. This already operates, with regional support, among those involved in staff development for PICKUP in FE colleges.

The future then, may lie in federal institutional structures – loose couplings of activities operating like shops in a mall – within federal national structures emphasizing the regional base within a federal Europe.

15

Management: Under New Management?

Robert Cuthbert

Introduction

Consider, for a moment, the images conjured up by the words 'new management'. For higher education in the early 1990s they have an ominous ring. For some academics, 'new management' will sound like a chapter from both Thatcher's and Orwell's 1984, conjuring up images of grey people newspeaking a language that the HE proles can barely understand or relate to their own experience. Yet for a small business 'under new management' is an advertising slogan, a triumphant declaration of fresh enthusiasm. For big business, new management is the currency of takeover talks, what bankers lend money for. Why should an activity so revered and prized in one sector be so despised in another?

The easy answer is that fundamental values differ. Universities are not like Union Carbide, and polytechnics are not driven by the profit motive. That easy answer is true, but inadequate. Worse, the easy answer threatens that which it purports to protect, the values and purposes of HE in a civilized society. The threat comes from the implied dismissal of 'management' as a useful tool or concept for HE. Colleges need to be managed just as much as commercial enterprises – managed differently, no doubt, but managed nevertheless. The communication of this message by successive government ministers during the 1980s has been severely distorted by the attendant reductions in real levels of spending per student, the accompanying political exhortations for ever more efficiency, and many academics' initial distaste for things managerial. The end of the 1980s sees morale and attitudes to management in British HE at a low ebb. Management, which has been part of the problem, must become part of the solution to the preservation of what is best in HE, as the system comes to terms with changing public assumptions about what HE is for, who should pay for it, and how much.

This chapter considers what needs to change, and what should stay the same, as new approaches to management in HE begin to reflect and to create a well-adjusted HE system for the twenty-first century. The mood of optimism will be sustained by evidence of emergent change, leading to speculation about the broad nature of that new system – under its new management.

Management, managers and managerialism

Some conceptual distinctions are necessary. 'Management' (perhaps better expressed as 'managing') I define as the process of getting things done, usually through the agency of other people – colleagues and employees (Cuthbert, 1984). All organizations are managed. The question is not whether management is a useful concept, but how management is conceived and how well it is executed in any particular organization. Managers are people who manage; this means most staff in universities and polytechnics. The focus of this chapter will be on broad patterns of management and thus, to some extent, on managers with broad, often institution-wide, responsibilities, but the second part case study shows also the key role of what McNay (1989a) calls 'activity managers' at lower levels in the hierarchy.

'Managerialism' is a particular and mistaken approach to managing, which purports to elevate the activity of managing above that which is managed, instead of recognizing that the two are inseparable parts of the same enterprise, and that each inevitably conditions the other. Managerialism is rightly derided as narrow (Raven, 1991) but sometimes wrongly confused with management itself; it is sometimes too easy to blame 'the management' when managers are actually making sincere efforts to grapple with moral dilemmas posed, for example, by financial cutbacks.

Why management must change

Of the changes charted elsewhere in this book, those most significant for HE management are the three interrelated and, I believe, irreversible changes in: (i) the legislative framework; (ii) levels of public financial support; and (iii) public attitudes towards HE. These changes affect other sectors, particularly FE, and much of what follows is transferable to those other contexts.

The Education Reform Act 1988

The effects of the 1988 ERA are still only slowly unfolding three years after the Act became law. The incorporation of the polytechnics and colleges which gained new legal independence continues to be widely welcomed as conferring a proper measure of institutional autonomy. The new Funding Councils have had very different experiences. The PCFC entered the vacuum created by the abolition of the local authorities' stake in HE, resolved to be noticeably different from its predecessor, the NAB. The PCFC's 'funding, not planning' role and its new funding methodology with its emphasis on competitive bidding have accentuated the inter-institutional competition for funds which was already a feature of the polytechnics and colleges sector. The UFC represented a less radical change from the UGC; its efforts to parallel the PCFC's funds bidding regime failed when its first major bidding exercise for the 1991–92 year was frustrated by almost all universities declining to cut 'prices' of student places below the UFC's own guide prices. Nevertheless the emergence of different bodies of opinion among vice-chancellors on, for example, the desirability of 'topping-up' fees above Government-recommended levels, shows how increased competitive pressures are also affecting the universities.

Contemporary journalistic judgements (Scott, 1990) reflect Whitehall opinion in contrasting the 'success' of PCFC with the 'failure' of the UFC in their early years. History may well view the precipitous fall in the PCFC unit of resource and the relative stability of the universities' unit rather differently: much will depend on the approaches adapted to the agenda outlined in Jennifer Bone's contribution (Chapter 4), in defining the role(s) of the 'new' HE system. However, the most significant legacy of the ERA is not likely to be the ultimately superficial changes in fortune in the superstructure of HE, but the heightened inter-institutional competition for students and funds, presaging greater institutional differentiation and diversity within an administratively simplified system.

Falling funding levels

These changes come after a prolonged period of financial stringency when it often seemed that government's question to HE was not 'what for?' but 'how much?'. Managers whose careers had developed in a climate of growth and concern for educational innovation had to learn how to manage contraction for efficiency and survival. At the same time demands for change by government, Funding Councils, students and employers accelerated. The typical polytechnic or college directorate had in the space of two short years to cope with the major change to corporate status (Cuthbert, 1988), the switch to a new funding system with completely unpredictable outcomes, virtually no capital investment, successive annual cuts of 5–10 per cent in the real level of spending per student, and a long-running major dispute between the new polytechnic and college employers and their academic staff. There are signs now, for whatever reason, of a resurgent focus on the 'what for?' question among HE managers.

Changing public attitudes to HE

In these circumstances the political demands for greater efficiency through wider use of market forces, which had seemed so insistent in the mid-1980s, were by 1990 receding in the consciousness of both government and institutional managers. Polytechnics were repeatedly labelled a 'success story' by

HE ministers, a commendation of understandably dubious merit in the eyes of many staff, who were at the sharp end of the productivity increases which made it possible to afford increasing access to HE. Universities, which had experienced an earlier period of adjustment, equally painful to their rawer sensibilities, were also more slowly coming to terms with the residue of Thatcherism: greater self-reliance; more competition; less public financial support but more funding from other sources; and staff disgruntled and demoralized because they felt persistently undervalued.

The 1988 Act was the high-water mark of 1980s' governments' concern to inject private sector management approaches into HE. The new HE corporations were required to have smaller Boards of Governors with a majority from 'industry, commerce, the professions and employment'. Yet the patronage afforded to the Secretary of State in appointing hundreds of these new Governors seemed likely to rebound as the new Board Chairs began to meet and agreed to lobby for much greater capital investment to support the ambitious access objectives set out by the Government.

The late 1980s also showed signs of change in the kind of higher education demanded by students. Credit accumulation and transfer systems (CATS) began to take hold as modular course structures became increasingly the norm in polytechnics and colleges. Flexibility and choice were in much demand as students sought HE opportunities which kept their career options open. The long-term implications of CATS will be revolutionary for institutions which have been accustomed to organizing themselves around mutually exclusive full-time and part-time modes of attendance by students, and a very limited range of programmed routes to defined final awards with few intermediate exit or re-entry points.

What needs to change, and what needs to stay the same

These environmental changes make changes in management inevitable. Paradoxically, such changes are necessary if certain underlying objectives and values are to stay the same – in those institutions where such continuity is indeed appropriate.

Managers must change or be changed. In the scramble to be ready for corporate status many in the PCFC sector appointed new kinds of senior manager, some from the universities, others from the private sector. As the initial 'shock of the new' subsided it became clearer that new kinds of expertise were indeed needed. The evidence of the long-running dispute with academic staff over pay and new contracts of employment suggested that employment relations expertise was most lacking, but early appointments emphasized financial and property management. At the top there was no more change than natural wastage implied, and it also became clear that much of the change would be in the attitudes and values of the managers rather than a change of personnel.

A parallel if more subtle change overtook the universities, coming to terms with the Jarratt Report (CVCP, 1985) and the changing demands of the new and much-criticized UFC. Jarratt had pointed out that the notion of the university vice chancellor as leading scholar, presiding over a loosely-coupled collection of basic units, was changing: 'The shift to the style of chief executive, bearing responsibility for ... effective management of the institution, is emerging ...'. The trickle of new pro-vice chancellor posts with explicit managerial responsibilities became a steady stream, and by mid-1990 an experienced American commentator (Martin, 1990) was suggesting that British universities would and should move rapidly towards USA and polytechnic models of institutional management, with a permanent pro-vice chancellor designated as the senior academic planner and policy development officer.

These changes in managers and managerial attitudes were accompanied by various structural changes, notably mergers within the PCFC sector and across the binary line to create new institutions. However, such restructuring, though no doubt potent in its effect on management, was often motivated by a quest either for survival or for higher (polytechnic or university) status, rather than being a deeper search for a new kind of HE institution with refashioned purposes and a new kind of management. Humberside and Bournemouth joined the polytechnic 'club' in 1990 just as most polytechnics anticipated leaving it to become universities, following the DES review of the Council for National Academic Awards. More significant was the quiet rescuing in 1990 by Polytechnic South West of the financially troubled Dartington College of Arts – evidence of the emerging regional responsibilities of larger institutions – and the imaginative proposal for association between Hatfield and Middlesex Polytechnics (Hatfield/Middlesex Polytechnics, 1990). Although soon called off after internal consultations, the proposed association might yet prove a harbinger of HE regrouping for the twenty-first century. The proposal was motivated explicitly by the intention to create a new kind of institution, in its size and scope more akin to American multi-campus state university systems than anything previously seen in the UK.

Such intentions were not, however, confined to the beneficiaries or victims of restructuring. Every university, polytechnic and college had been required in the late 1980s by its funding body to create and report on its strategic plan. Although the self-conscious emphasis on 'missions' and 'visions' initially spawned many platitudes and statements of the obvious, real differences in institutional mission slowly became more explicit. The voluntary colleges had led the way, showing how a particular academic philosophy and particular values could be reflected in every aspect of the college's management (Gay *et al.*, 1986). In universities the abortive but persistent 'R, X or T' debate about involvement in research forced a wider reappraisal of institutional roles and prospects. Polytechnics and colleges began to position themselves differently despite rather than because of the PCFC's bizarre attempts to simulate a market by driving down course 'prices' to lowest common denominator levels.

Some staff and students saw in these developments nothing but further evidence of the rise of what might be called the 'managerialist tendency', characterized by a concern for public relations rather than public service. Yet there is scope for optimism that this emphasis on mission and distinctive purposes will help reaffirm some core values – concern for students and their personal development, for knowledge and the pursuit of learning for its own sake, but also for the application of knowledge to worthy practical purposes. It is becoming increasingly clear that not every institution can be all of these things to all people. In the 1990s HE institutions will increasingly choose explicitly to serve only some people, and some purposes, within a comprehensive overall system.

The challenge for managers is to help their institution to identify the mission which is right for their students and potential students, their staff and the wider society. To discover what the changes might mean for management within the institution the final part of this chapter will consider a case study of one institution's development of a new approach to management to suit its new circumstances.

Changing the managerial culture at Bristol Polytechnic

Too often, people caught up in some intensely topical change are embarrassed at the 'revolutionary' label they give at the time to what turns out to be the merest blip in institutional evolution. Care is needed, then, in making grand assertions about cultural change, even in one institution. Let me say first what is *not* changing. Despite many claims to the contrary, disciplinary cultures (in Becher's (1989) sense) seem to be surviving the onslaught of deep cuts in the unit of resource. I offer no evidence, other than the continuation of research, scholarship, and new course development which I take as basic signs of healthy disciplines, and their normal concomitant, the emergence of new disciplines. Disciplinary cultures, deep-rooted in decades if not centuries of growth, may prove to be more resilient than the delivery modes which have been the late twentieth century norm but are now breaking up under the same onslaught. (The basic pattern of lecture-plus-tutorial is now being substantially modified as people and institutions adopt more flexible, accessible and open course structures and teaching/learning strategies.) However, institutions' managerial cultures – the set of attitudes, values and shared understandings which constitute and are constituted by managerial action – are more fragile and evanescent than their basic units' cultures. To say that the managerial culture is changing is therefore a more modest claim. For an illustration, consider recent changes at Bristol Polytechnic, which I can describe from personal experience.

The Polytechnic Directorate took the view early in the new HE corporation's life in 1988 that legal and financial independence called for a different approach to academic leadership and management. An early sense of the need for change was only partly focused by the development of a strategic plan in response to the promptings of PCFC (Bristol Polytechnic, 1989). The plan involved a linked set of changes in staffing, physical and financial resources, and in organization structures and teaching/learning strategies, all designed to preserve what was seen as the Polytechnic's leading position as a high-quality provider of polytechnic higher education.

Even the first plan in 1989 envisaged a change in management through a new planning process and the creation of 'contracts', later relabelled 'planning agreements' between the Directorate and the major teaching departments. First, though, came the necessary infrastructure changes following the assumption of corporate status – new financial management and information systems, restructuring academic support services, and the regrouping and development of personnel, property, secretarial and legal services. The introduction of planning agreements was meant to change attitudes, reorient middle managers' attention towards outcomes, and clarify targets as a basis for subsequent performance review. The agreements were conceived as short (two-page) statements of key short-term priorities for each department, set within the context of the Polytechnic strategic plan and against the backdrop of longer-term departmental and faculty development plans. The process of reaching agreement was probably more important than the agreements themselves in unifying previously separate discussions about budgets, course intakes, staffing complements, new course development and so on. As one internal document put it:

> This is not meant in any way to weaken the emphasis on the academic and educational dimension, nor is it meant to inhibit academic diversity. Rather it aims to put educational objectives in the context of financial possibilities – to balance quality and cost. This means that managers at all levels will be expected to take a rounded view of performance against targets, to balance achievements against costs, and to compare income with expenditure. They will have more responsibility and more freedom to manage, but they will be held to account for overall performance – the balance between quality and cost – *on the bottom line*.
>
> (Bristol Polytechnic, 1990)

The changes were thus conceived as making the financial dimension of performance much more prominent, and giving middle managers more autonomy and devolved authority, balanced by more stress on accountability. The transformation of the managerial culture developed in parallel in several dimensions, which can be described in terms of structure, process, outcomes and focus.

Alongside the initial infrastructure changes came a restructuring of Directorate responsibilities which mirrored PCFC's organizational division between Programmes and Resources, recognizing the Funding Council as the single most important external influence on the Polytechnic. Support services were regrouped and became explicitly responsible to one or other of three Deputy Directors. In resource management the changes aimed to support the increased responsibility and independence of heads of teaching departments, promoting a transition *from centralization to decentralization.* In the academic dimension (Programmes) the restructuring of central services aimed to support the declared learning strategy, emphasizing flexible and open learning systems. There was thus a planned shift *from autonomy to interdependence* for the basic academic planning units. These shifts in different directions amounted to structural convergence on a position of considerable independence, albeit within a tightly coupled system.

The change in internal processes was no less marked. Before incorporation the Polytechnic's dependence on its local authority had been mirrored by an internal dependence of departments on the centre. Management processes reflected this: the LEA provided no worthwhile financial management information to the Polytechnic, and the centre did likewise for the departments. New financial systems turned this situation upside down. Income, formerly treated as accruing to the Polytechnic and disbursed to the departments, became treated as accruing to the teaching departments, and 'taxed' to support central services. Departments knew for the first time the income attributed to their activities as well as the costs of those activities. Support divisions provide a service to the departments and the cost of that service has become known, and its basis negotiable. The move to explicit planning agreements as public documents aimed to seal a transition from covert 'deals' to overt agreements, an intended transition *from closed to open styles of management.*

The development of planning agreements also helped to shift attention to the relationships between income, budget and outcomes and the need to manage all three together. Where feedback on middle managers' performance had been diffuse it promised to become much clearer – a transition *from ambiguity to clarity of expected performance.* Consistent with this and the other changes, and strongly pressed by most if not all external influences on the Polytechnic, was a changed orientation, a transition *from focus on process to focus on outcomes.*

These various changes led to what it is reasonable to call a change in managerial culture, to a position in which clear targets for performance would be set by relatively open negotiations, giving managers more freedom and responsibility for achievement, monitoring their performance and holding them explicitly accountable for both academic and financial results. Another way of seeing the change was as an attempt to strengthen strategic management at the level of the department. Pre-existing development plans were couched in largely operational terms, describing courses to be developed and projecting student and staff numbers, often with a five–ten year horizon. The new Polytechnic strategic plan aimed to provide a sense of corporate direction and mission, with only a three-year planning horizon. Planning agreements were designed to fill the gap at middle management

Table 15.1 The cultural transition in Bristol Polytechnic

	Past		Present		Future
Structures:					
Resources	Centralized	→	Devolving	→	Decentralized
Programmes	Autonomous	→	Collaborating	→	Interdependent
Processes	Closed	→	Emerging	→	Open
Expected Performance	Ambiguous	→	Negotiating	→	Clear
Focus	Process	→	Reorienting	→	Outcomes
Culture	Dependence	→	Learning	→	Independence

level, initially looking forward only one year. The future development of the process will aim for longer planning horizons at middle and corporate levels so as explicitly to strengthen the Polytechnic's strategic management.

Summary: The cultural transition

The changes at Bristol are represented in Table 15.1. They may be characterized as an overall transition *from dependence to independence*. The retrospective account of recent changes tidies up more than it should the messy and confused process which is most people's experience of institutions coping with these kinds of change. Financial devolution, more academic collaboration and greater managerial accountability are on every institutional agenda in the early 1990s. It remains to be seen whether these become more than passing fads, an anachronistic echo of Thatcherism. I believe the change will be permanent, and beneficial for HE because it contains the seeds of a more diverse HE system, in which the binary and other lines disappear to allow different institutions to pursue different purposes, untrammelled by arbitrary administrative distinctions with built-in financial discrimination. In response to external and internal changes HE managers will inevitably, and increasingly willingly, begin to operate on the basis of different assumptions about what management is for and how it should be accomplished. There is no reason to be pessimistic about the prospect. HE should learn to celebrate its new management as the protector of excellence in diversity.

16

The World: Post-compulsory Education and the International Community

John Othick

In one of his first pronouncements as the Open University's new Vice-Chancellor, Dr John Daniel, asked whether the University can 'think globally' and thus become the first 'global university'. His speech was replete with reminders that educators and their institutions inhabit a rapidly changing international context. The challenge is not just to accommodate to global change, but to influence its course and outcomes. This chapter explores the nature and origins of this changing global context; it asks if an international 'community of educators' is likely to emerge; and it addresses the question of whose interests such a community might serve.

The balance between continuity and change has been one theme in this book. These cannot be counterposed as alternatives. In the international context, continuity is likely to produce change: many trends established in the 1980s will continue through the 1990s, but their outcomes might well be different. It is essential to outline the key changes that have transformed the world scene and to assess how they have affected post-compulsory education. An historical perspective is unavoidable if meaningful judgements are to be made about future trends.

For many people, the 1980s will be remembered as the time when the Iron Curtain crumbled as Thatcherism and AIDS spread like epidemics; and as years of heightened awareness of the environment, of poverty, and of famine. These relatively new concerns were superimposed on a background of continuity: the North remained obdurate in its refusal to recognize its responsibilities towards the South; the revolution in communications technology continued apace; international co-operation in Europe and North America went from strength to strength. Each of these processes was affected by one or more of the others. All had a significant international dimension. They combined to create new demands, expectations and trends in relation to post-compulsory education.

It is important to recognize that education already had an established role within the international community before these changes occurred. The contemporary world has been moulded not just by the international flow of goods, capital, and people, but also by the long-standing spread of ideas, skills, institutions, technology and culture. Diffusion took place often within a few years or decades, and always to a range of very different societies. Its pace accelerated over time; its impact varied from one society to another. Educators always played a key role in generating and disseminating knowledge within a global market where need rarely translated into effective demand. It was a form of supply-side education, where providers judged demand according to their own criteria rather than those of the clients. It became an instrument of imperialism, as whole societies were required to learn and live by the culture of their rulers. These were the antecedents of the processes which now appear to impel us towards the global university. How far, and for what reasons, has all this changed in the more recent past?

Technology has advanced and institutional structures have evolved in ways which now permit more rapid transmission of information. Political and economic imperatives have led to inter-governmental co-operation on an unprecedented scale. These processes continue to produce significant re-alignment of interests. Developed countries have increasingly interacted with one another rather than with their erstwhile colonies. The end of the Cold War looks likely to further isolate the underdeveloped world as the West looks to the East. One consequence of these trends during the 1980s was the spread of Thatcherite ideas and policies, particularly within the developed world.

Educators were generally under pressure from government to become more 'relevant' and efficient. Institutions had to be run along more managerial lines. Courses and programmes became products to be marketed; students became consumers or clients; alumni became potential benefactors. Relations with business and with funding agencies became closer yet more instrumental. Evaluation, assessment, and appraisal became established processes. Development and training were offered to help transform staff perspectives. Above all, failure to recognize these imperatives became more problematic as jobs became less secure.

The forces of the market place permeated the world of post-compulsory education from below as well as from above. The expectations of learners had to adjust to the harsh realities of a world where dole queues had become a permanent feature. Demand-led policies had to accommodate to the needs of a more discerning clientele faced with a widening range of alternatives. Demographic trends ensured that more women and older people became learners, and that their needs had to be assessed and met. Recognition and accreditation of prior learning and experience were increasingly required. Employment trends signified greater emphasis on re-training and on skills updating. Distinctions between students and employees became more blurred as business put money into placements, sponsorship, day release or in-house staff development. Institutions became more accountable not just to learners but also to those who paid their fees.

The upshot of such trends was a crucial paradox: educators and institutions were inevitably forced to compete in order to attract students and funding; yet they were simultaneously urged to rationalize their activities through co-operation. These twin processes were increasingly evident both within and between institutions. Individuals and departments had to co-operate in order to compete more effectively with other groups for scarce research funding. Institutions had to compete with each other to secure closer co-operation with outside agencies and business.

Impelled by similar pressures, institutions in each society increasingly had to compete in a global market. They were producing graduates who needed to be internationally mobile. They were seeking closer co-operation with firms that operated on a multi-national basis. Inevitably, attention focused on the quality of both the process and its outcome: that is, educational programmes had to measure up to those available in other countries; and graduates were expected to acquire skills that would compare with those being developed elsewhere.

The idea that international standards had to be applied was adopted by the Committee of Vice-Chancellors and Principals (CVCP) in its 1988 paper on *The British PhD*. They argued that British practice must come more into line with that in other countries, particularly in regard to the inclusion of 'taught components' and of language training. Their purpose was clearly to ensure that the British 'product' could compete internationally. The insistence of CVCP on external evaluation was similarly evident in the establishment of its Academic Audit Unit. Once educators are required to strive for quality control and assurance, it is difficult to see how this can be achieved without reference to a common currency of international standards.

Institutions were similarly required to look to the global market place for funding and students. The EC has become an increasingly important source of support for research, though this clearly entails international competition. Alumni associations proliferate as universities on this side of the Atlantic seek the support of graduates who have prospered in North America. My own institution is typical in having set up a new External Relations Committee, and in strengthening the role of its International Liaison Officer. The establishment of student and staff exchanges and the attraction of international conferences have become a routine aspect of the business. Individual units are exhorted to exploit international opportunities: computer science students are sent on placements to Germany and Japan; distance learning programmes provide training in pharmacy for learners in the Middle East. Overseas students are courted with great vigour for the handsome fees they bring in.

As educators and their institutions moved more firmly into the international arena, their efforts were characterized by anything from amateur enthusiasm to polished professionalism. Either way, they entered an environment where fundamental inequalities already existed. Through no choice of their own, institutions naturally focused attention on those who could pay for their services, and those who might provide funds. For those in less developed regions this was not encouraging. To be sure, things had changed from the days of empire: then, we decided what the colonial élites needed; now the élites are free to pay for whatever they want. Educators have thus in many instances reinforced an international status quo inherited from history. One of the major challenges of the 1990s is for education to become a more powerful instrument for reducing international inequalities.

The evidence from the 1980s suggests that the capacity exists to transform education into a force for liberation and empowerment, but that political constraints tend to inhibit this. Historically, it has always been convenient to assume that what was good for the developed world must automatically be good for less developed regions. This meant the implantation of attitudes and institutional structures which were often inappropriate to the needs of the society concerned. In one sense, the hegemony of Thatcherism served to undermine this tradition, which had been sustained in part through international student mobility. In the Commonwealth, in particular, there had for decades been a steady flow of able students coming to colleges and universities in countries such as Britain and Canada. By the 1980s, there was considerable concern that sharp fee rises had severely reduced this form of student mobility. The reasons for these anxieties provide valuable insights into the dilemmas which surround the role of education in the international economy.

During the early 1980s, other industrialized countries such as France and West Germany were beginning to show an interest in attracting students from less developed regions of the Commonwealth. It might be expected that this would have been seen as a welcome development by everyone, in that it meant that benefits would still flow to underdeveloped countries via this particular educational mechanism. But, on the contrary, concern was expressed that Britain and Canada would lose out if Commonwealth students continued to go elsewhere. In short, the link created through student mobility was deemed to be of great advantage to the host countries as well as to the poorer members of the Commonwealth. The benefits to countries such as Britain lay in the business and political links which were perpetuated. Student mobility was a way of training a managerial and professional élite who, when in positions of power and influence, would return the favours they had previously received from the host countries.

The extent to which the poorer nations benefited from this process is unclear. According to the perspective adopted, education is seen as an agency for modernization, or as an instrument for perpetuating dependency. There was clearly a growing need for technical and managerial know-how as these countries struggled to industrialize. On the other hand, critics hold that striving to emulate western patterns of development was a mistake: less developed countries would have been better to follow their own path, with their own distinctive educational and institutional structures. Participants at a UNESCO consultation in April 1991 were also concerned about the non-return on investment from sponsored third-world students. Many did not return but were recruited by the institutions where they went to study. A brain-drain thus siphoned off the best talent from South to North. The argument has since taken on another dimension, and it is this that seems likely to become one of the major debates of the 1990s.

One response to this by developing countries and to the fall in overseas student enrolments in Britain because of imposed fee levels was the idea that distance education could become an alternative: technological advance made it possible for programmes to be delivered to learners in their home countries. One result was the establishment of the Commonwealth of Learning towards the end of the 1980s. Its remit was to act as a co-ordinating agency through which existing distance education institutions throughout the Commonwealth would co-operate. Like student mobility before it, the Commonwealth of Learning seems on the surface to be a well-intentioned initiative through which more affluent member states will contribute to the educational and developmental needs of the less fortunate. But some important issues are raised which will need to be resolved during the 1990s. Whether we really are moving towards global educational provision, and for whose benefit, will depend very much on how they are resolved.

Perhaps the most fundamental issue is whether the resources will be there to allow an institution such as the Commonwealth of Learning to evolve into an effective agency for co-ordinating the delivery of education on a global scale. The evidence so far is not very promising. Funding was provided for a limited time-scale, with the largest contributions coming from Canada and the UK (in that order). Significantly, quite large contributions have been made by relatively poor countries such as Nigeria, whereas comparatively small ones have come from affluent societies like Australia. Some of the largest contributors have signalled that their commitment cannot be depended on in the long term, and that they expect the institution to attract more funding from private sources. The implications of this are not encouraging, particularly if it is recalled that many other providers are already operating internationally. For example, a consortium of FE colleges in the north of England does business worth several million pounds a year based on learning packages for Malaysia and Singapore; the University of Hull offers an MBA in Hong Kong supported by staff visits once every 2 months; the Open University franchises courses for use in East Asia. Satellite broadcasting allows multi-national companies to transmit programmes to work-based learning centres world-wide. Company-labelled higher degrees through tutored-video-instruction already exist in the USA.

Because they are driven by market considerations, these activities tend to reinforce existing inequalities. An institution such as the Commonwealth of Learning therefore needs adequate funding simply to be able to counteract the trends which already exist because of the activities of other providers. If it is forced down the same path as them, it cannot be expected to achieve results radically different from theirs.

The resource issue leaves us with two rather depressing, but quite likely, scenarios: one is the emergence of a quasi-global institution made impotent by under-funding. Alternatively, it could be forced into the mould inherited from the 1980s, and achieve little other than the perpetuation of the status quo. There is another possibility: that resources will be released on a scale which will make it a viable venture. But this rather depends on the strength of competing demands, which raises the second basic issue concerning the globalization of learning: would there be a substantial cost which would fall on other areas of provision?

If it seems likely that resources would be made available, but only by cutting back elsewhere, debates would naturally arise as to whether this would be justifiable. I see two types of debate, both of which could lead to various scenarios. One is about whether charity and openness should begin at home. There is a strong view that, in spite of all the efforts of recent years to open up post-compulsory education, much still needs to be done to facilitate access and to equalize opportunity and perhaps outcomes. The most urgent priority is to get things right at home so as to evolve a model which might be more appropriate for exporting. In this view, any attempt to divert funds away from these purposes would be strongly resisted. In the OU this has been true over its outreach to Europe, with students and the DES for once making common cause.

The other area of debate will probably concern the issue of whether attempts at internationalization should be general and ambitious, or whether they should be more targeted and perhaps practical. From a British perspective, this is most obviously a debate about Europe versus the world. So far, the evidence is that Europe is the firm favourite: 1992 is already indelibly imprinted in people's minds as a significant year in the future of Europe rather than as a fairly important anniversary in the history of the New World. Already, so many institutions have committed so much to securing for themselves an educational role within the expanding EC. It is difficult to see that there could be any significant diversion of resources away from this kind of venture without powerful protest.

Both types of debate suggest scenarios for the 1990s of continuing conflict over resource allocation, with fully international initiatives looking probable losers. One other angle on this concerns the role of the Open University. John Daniel played a key role in the establishment of the Commonwealth of Learning, but the OU has recently exhibited more enthusiasm for Europe than for the Commonwealth. This will almost certainly continue, in spite of the Vice-Chancellor's comments about the University seeking out 'thrilling opportunities' in the developing world. The relationship with the Commonwealth of Learning does not seem to have been particularly close or comfortable, though Dr Daniel is presumably better placed than most people to change this. Collaboration would suggest an optimistic scenario, though even competition could generate creative tension which would accelerate globalization. Either way, the key issue would be what kind of global provision they were seeking to create.

This raises a third critical issue which will be debated, though probably not resolved, in the next decade. Even if resources are plentiful, and if institutional and governmental commitment is genuine, this does not guarantee the emergence of global educational provision which is consistent with global educational needs. Although it might seem to be a panacea, distance learning is not without problems when used in a developmental context. It can be costly to set up, requiring extensive and efficient telecommunications infrastructure. It may require a level of private ownership of consumer goods which is in fact beyond the reach of those whose needs are greatest. It carries risks of imposing external culture and language, and thus stifling the expression of local and regional distinctiveness. Such risks can engender hostility or provoke competition. It is significant that an international Francophone distance learning system now operates from Canada, and that it is attempting to establish networks with other foreign language providers throughout Latin America. None of the above is a reason for not encouraging globalization to proceed; but all of them are reasons why it should proceed cautiously and with due regard to needs.

This could happen in the 1990s, but that would probably be excessively optimistic. The contemporary world economy is characterized by deep and enduring inequalities. It has increasing mobility of technology, skills, knowledge and the people who have ownership of these outcomes of education; yet, on the other hand, it has static concentrations of deprivation, confined to islands from which there seems little chance of escape. Global institutions or other forms of international provision could no doubt do much to change this. But that, I feel, is something which is unlikely to occur in the 1990s.

Bibliography

Alverno College Faculty (1989). *Liberal Learning at Alverno College*, Milwaukee, Alverno College Productions.

Annan, N. (1970). 'The University and the intellect'. *Times Literary Supplement*, 3557.

Arrowsmith, B. (1990). *The Distribution of the College Budget After the Implementation of the Education Reform Act*, Sheffield, Training Agency/Dudley College.

Association of Metropolitan Authorities (1990a). *Further Education: Towards Coherence – a Brief for Decision Makers*, London, AMA.

Association of Metropolitan Authorities (1990b). *Education in Europe*, London, AMA.

Atkinson, J. and Meager, N. (1986). *New Forms of Work Organisation*, Brighton, Institute of Manpower Studies.

Audit Commission (1985). *Obtaining Better Value from Further Education*, London, HMSO.

Audit Commission (1990). *We Can't Go On Meeting Like This*, London, HMSO.

Ball, C. (1990). *More Means Different*, London, RSA.

Barnett, C. (1975). 'FE and the development of an industrial society'. *Coombe Lodge Report* 8 (14).

Becher, T. (1987). 'Staffing and academic structure'. In T. Becher (ed.) *British Higher Education*, London, Allen & Unwin.

Becher, T. (1989). *Academic Tribes and Territories*, Milton Keynes, Open University Press.

Becher, T. and Kogan, M. (1992). *Process and Structure in Higher Education*, London, Heinemann.

Bevan, J. (1988). 'Incorporation and Assisted Status or Not?'. In M. Kedney and D.L. Parkes (eds) *Implications of the 1988 Education Reform Act*, London, FEU.

Birch, D. (1988). *Managing Resources in Further Education, A Handbook for College Managers*, Blagdon, Further Education Staff College.

Birch, W. (1988). *The Challenge to Higher Education: Reconciling Responsibilities to Scholarship and to Society*, Milton Keynes, SRHE/Open University Press.

Bristol Polytechnic (1989). *Mission and Strategy 1989*, June, mimeo.

Bristol Polytechnic (1990). *The Bottom Line*, Report by the Head of Corporate Planning, October, mimeo.

Brunskill, I. (1990). *The Regeneration Game: A Regional Approach to Regional Policy*, London, Institute for Public Policy Research.

Bruton (1987). 'University planning and management in conditions of complexity and uncertainty'. *Higher Education Quarterly* 41 (4).

Cambridgeshire County Council (1989). *Implications for the FE Sector. Cambridgeshire 1992 Project*, Vol. 3, Cambridgeshire County Council.

Cassels, J. (1990). *Britain's Real Skill Shortage and What to Do About it*, Exeter, Policy Studies Institute.

Cerych, L. and Sabatier, P. (1986). *Great Expectations and Mixed Performance: The Implementation of Higher Education Reforms in Europe*, London, Trentham Books.

Chin, R. and Benne, K.D. (1976). 'General strategies for effecting changes in human systems'. In W.G. Bennis *et al.* (eds) *The Planning of Change*, New York, Holt, Rinehart & Winston.

Cohen, M.D. and March, J.G. (1983). 'Leadership and ambiguity'. In O. Boyd-Barrett *et al.* (eds) *Approaches to Post-school Management*, London, Harper & Row.

Commission of the European Communities (1990). *Establishing an Action Programme for the Development of Continuing Vocational Training in the EC*, (FORCE), 6276/90, EC.

Committee of Directors of Polytechnics/Committee of Vice-Chancellors and Principals (1990). *Financing the Expansion of Higher Education*, London, CDP/CVCP.

Committee of Vice-Chancellors and Principals (1985). *Report of the Steering Committee for Efficiency Studies in Universities*, London, CVCP (The Jarratt Report).

Committee of Vice-Chancellors and Principals (1988). *The British PhD*, London, CVCP.

Conference of University Administrators (1978). *Report of the Group on Forecasting and University Expansion*, Norwich, CUA.

Council for Industry and Higher Education (1987). *Towards a Partnership: Higher Education – Government – Industry*, London, CIHE.

Council for National Academic Awards (1990). *Directory of CNAA First Degree and Undergraduate Courses, 1990–91*, London, CNAA.

Curry, A.M. (1989). 'The psychology of restrictions to access'. Paper presented at the SRHE Annual Conference.

Cuthbert, R.E. (1984). *The Management Process, E324. Management in Postcompulsory Education*, Block 3 Part 2, Milton Keynes, Open University.

Cuthbert, R.E. (1988). *Going Corporate*, Blagdon, The Further Education Staff College.

Dearing, R. (1989). 'Sector Strategy'. Speech to the PCFC Annual Conference.

de Jouvenel, H. (1988). *Etude preliminaire sur le vieillissement démographic en Europe: les activités des personnes agées*, Council of Europe.

Deloitte, Haskins, Sells (1987). *The Funding of Vocational Education and Training*, Sheffield, MSC.

Department of Education and Science (1966). *A Plan for Polytechnics and Other Colleges: Higher Education in the Further Education System*, Cmnd 3006, London, HMSO.

Department of Education and Science (1972). *Education: A Framework for Expansion*, Cm 5174, London, HMSO.

Department of Education and Science (1974). *Development of Higher Education in the Non-University Sector: Interim Arrangements for the Control of Advanced Courses*, DES Circular 6/74.

Department of Education and Science (1978). *Report of the Working Group on the Management of Higher Education in the Public Sector*, London, HMSO.

Department of Education and Science (1986). *The Development of Higher Education into the 1990s*, Cmnd 9524, London, HMSO.

Department of Education and Science (1987a). *Higher Education: Meeting the Challenge*, Cm 114, London, HMSO.

170   *Visions of Post-compulsory Education*

Department of Education and Science (1987b). *Managing Colleges Efficiently*, London, HMSO.
Department of Education and Science (1989a). *Aspects of Higher Education in the USA. A commentary by HMI*, London, HMSO.
Department of Education and Science (1989b). *The English Polytechnics, An HMI Commentary*, London, HMSO.
Department of Education and Science (1989c). *Further Education: A New Strategy*, Speech by Kenneth Baker, Secretary of State, London, HMSO.
Department of Education and Science (1989d). *Top-up Loans for Students*, London, HMSO.
Department of Education and Science (1990). *Education and Economic Activity of Young People aged 16 to 18 years in England from 1975 to 1990*, Statistical Bulletin 9/90, London, DES.
Department of Education and Science/PICKUP (1989). *After Lancaster House*, London, FEU/PICKUP.
Department of Education, Northern Ireland (1982). *The Future of Higher Education in Northern Ireland*, Belfast, HMSO.
Department of Employment (1984). *Training for Jobs*, Cmnd 9135, London, HMSO.
Department of Employment (1990). Press release on launch of training credits, 27 March.
Duke, C. (1987). *The Future Shape of Continuing Education and Universities*, Papers in Continuing Education 1, University of Warwick.
EDUCA (1986). *College Management – The Demands of the 1990s*. Issue 68, December.
European Community (1989a). *Education and Training in the European Community: Guidelines for the Medium Term, 1989–1992*, COM (89) 236, EC.
European Community (1989b). 'Education in the Run-up to 1993'. *CEDEFOP News*, No. 5.
European Community (1990). *Education and Training*, Vol. O, December.
Eurich, N.P. (1985). *Corporate Classrooms: The Learning Business*, Princeton, NJ, Princeton University Press for The Carnegie Foundation for the Advancement of Learning.
Fielden, J. (1990). 'The shifting culture of higher education'. In P.W.G. Wright (ed.) *Industry and Higher Education*, Milton Keynes, SRHE/Open University Press.
Finegold, D. and Soskice, D. (1988). 'The failure of training in Britain: analysis and prescription'. *Oxford Review of Economic Policy* 4 (2).
Fonda, N. and Hayes, C. (1988). 'Education, training and business performance'. *Oxford Review of Economic Policy* 5 (3).
Fox, S. (1989). 'The production and distribution of knowledge through open and distance learning'. *Educational and Training Technology International* 26(3).
Further Education Unit (1986). *A Fragmented View?* London, FEU.
Further Education Unit (1987). *Relevance, Flexibility and Competence*, London, FEU.
Further Education Unit (1989). *Towards an Educational Audit*, London, FEU.
Further Education Unit (1990). 'Performance indicators in the education and training of adults'. *FEU Bulletin*, June.
Garratt, R. (1987). *The Learning Organization*, London, Fontana/Collins.
Gay, J. *et al.* (1986). *The Future of the Anglican Colleges*, Abingdon, Culham College Institute.
Gelpi, E. (1990). 'Community, education and migrant workers: myths and realities'. In C. Poster and A. Kruger (eds) *Community Education in the Western World*, London, Routledge.

Gordon, J. (1989). *Comparative Study of Qualifications at the end of Compulsory Education, Secondary Education and Vocational Training: UK Study*, Brussels, European Commission.

Griffiths, J. (1989). *Universities and the State: The Next Steps*, London, Campaign for Academic Freedom and Democracy.

Guttman, A. (1987). *Democratic Education*, Princeton, NJ, Princeton University Press.

Halsey, A.H. (1985). 'The idea of a university'. *Oxford Review of Education* 11.

Handy, C.B. (1983). 'The organizations of consent'. In O. Boyd-Barrett *et al.* (eds) *Approaches to Post-School Management*, London, Harper & Row.

Handy, C. (1989). *The Age of Unreason*, London, Business Books.

Hatfield/Middlesex Polytechnics (1990). *Report of Joint Working Group*, November, mimeo.

Hayes, C. (1988a). *Strategies and People*, Brighton, The Prospect Centre.

Hayes, C. (1988b). *An Integrated Vocational Education and Training System for the Future*, London, FEU.

Her Majesty's Inspectors (1986). *Adult Education in Sheffield*, London, DES.

HMSO (1985). *The Development of Higher Education into the 1990s*, Cmnd 9524, London, HMSO.

HMSO (1990). *Highly Qualified People: Supply and Demand*, Report of an Interdepartmental Review, London, HMSO.

HMSO (1991a). *Access and Opportunity: A Strategy for Education and Training*, Cm 1530, Edinburgh, HMSO.

HMSO (1991b). *Education and Training for the 21st Century*, Cm 1536, London, HMSO (two volumes).

HMSO (1991c). *Higher Education: A New Framework*, Cm 1541, London, HMSO.

Hoggart, R. (1990). *A Sort of Clowning*, London, Chatto & Windus.

Holland, G. (1985). *After Competence and Competition.* Policy paper to MSC, Sheffield.

Hooper, R. (1977). *National Development Programme in Computer Assisted Learning.* Final report of the Director. London, Council for Educational Technology.

Hooper, R. and Toye, I. (1975). *Computer Assisted Learning in the United Kingdom: Some Case Studies*, London, Council for Educational Technology.

Institute for Public Policy and Research (1990). *A British Baccalaureat*, London, IPPR.

James Report (1972). *Teacher Education and Training.* A Report by a Committee of Inquiry appointed by the Secretary of State for Education and Science, under the Chairmanship of Lord James of Rusholme, London, HMSO.

Jaspers, K. (1960). *The Idea of the University*, London, Peter Owen.

Johnson, R. (1990). Report in *IPM Journal*, June.

Kahne, H. (1988). *Reconceiving Part-time Work*, Totowa, NJ, Rowman & Allan.

Kerr, C. (1963). *The Uses of the University*, Cambridge, MA, Harvard University Press.

Kulich, J. (1985). 'Training of adult educators in East European countries'. *Convergence* XVIII, No. 3–4.

Labour Party (1990). *Looking to the Future*, London, Labour Party.

Lauglo, J. (1977). 'Education change and aspects of bureaucratic organisation'. In R. Glatter (ed.) *Control of the Curriculum: Issues and Trends in Britain and Europe*, Slough, NFER.

Lauglo, J. and Lillis, K. (eds) (1988). *Vocationalizing Education: An International Perspective*, Oxford, Pergamon.

Legge, D. (1985). 'Training of adult education workers in West Europe'. *Convergence* XVIII, No. 3–4.

Lindop Report (1985). *Academic Validation in Public Sector Higher Education.* Report of the Committee of enquiry into the academic validation of degree courses in public sector higher education, chaired by Sir Norman Lindop. April, Cmnd 9501, London, HMSO.

Lockwood, G. (1987). 'The management of universities'. In T. Becher (ed.) *British Higher Education*, London, Allen & Unwin.

Lyotard, J.F. (1984). *The Postmodern Condition: A Report on Knowledge*, Minneapolis, University of Minnesota Press.

MacGregor, J. (1990). *Bloomfield Memorial Lecture*, Portsmouth Polytechnic.

McNay, I. (1989a). *Coping with Crisis*, London, Longman for FEU.

McNay, I. (1989b). *The Reality of College Management*, London, Longman for FEU.

McNay, I. (1991). 'Cooperation, coordination and quality in employer and education partnerships: a role for the regions'. In P. Raggatt and L. Unwin (eds) *Change and Intervention: Vocational Education and Training*, Lewes, Falmer Press.

Manpower Services Commission (1981a). *The New Training Initiative: An Agenda for Action*, Cmnd 8455, London, HMSO.

Manpower Services Commission (1981b). *A New Training Initiative: A Consultative Document*, Sheffield, MSC.

Martin, J. (1990). 'More gown, less town'. *Times Higher Education Supplement*, 29 June.

Martin, L. (1985). 'The funding of continuing education for adults with special reference to the Replan programme'. *Studies in the Education of Adults* 17(2).

Meyer-Dohm, P. (1990). 'Graduates of Higher Education: what do employers expect in the 1990s?' In P.W.G. Wright (ed.) *Industry and Higher Education*, Milton Keynes, SRHE/Open University Press.

Miller, J. *et al.* (1986). *Preparing for Change*, London, Longman for FEU.

Ministry of Education (1957). *The Scope and Content of the Three Year Course of Teacher Training: Sixth Report of the National Advisory Committee on the Training and Supply of Teachers*, London, HMSO.

National Audit Office (1987). *Adult Training Strategy*, London, HMSO.

National Economic Development Office/Manpower Services Commission (1984). *Competence and Competition*, London, NEDO.

National Economic Development Office/Training Commission (1988). *Young People and the Labour Market: A Challenge for The 1990s*, London, NEDO.

National Institute for Economic and Social Research (1989). *Productivity, Education and Training: Britain and Other Countries Compared*, London, NIESR.

Neave, G. (1988). 'On the cultivation of quality, efficiency and enterprise. An overview of recent trends in higher education in Western Europe, 1986–88'. *European Journal of Education* 23(1/2).

Northern Ireland Ministry of Education (1965). *Higher Education in Northern Ireland*, Belfast, HMSO.

Oglesby, K.L. (1989). *Valkenburg Report*, Amersfoort, EBAE.

Oglesby, K.L. (1991). 'Staff development for adult educators: European aspects'. *Adults Learning* 2(5).

O'Hear, A. (1988). 'Academic freedom and the university'. In M. Tight (ed.) *Academic Freedom and Responsibility*, Milton Keynes, SRHE/Open University Press.

Parkes, D.L. and Shaw, G.K. (1983). 'Britons take a Meister class'. *Times Higher Educational Supplement*, 24 August.

Patterson, W. (1983). *Nuclear Power*, Harmondsworth, Penguin.

Paxman, J. (1990). *Friends in High Places: Who runs Britain?* London, Michael Joseph.

Pedler, M., Boydell, T. and Burgoyne, J. (1989). 'Towards the learning company'. *Management Education and Development* 20(1).

Peters, T.J. and Waterman, R.H. (1982). *In Search of Excellence*, New York, Harper & Row.

Phillimore, A.J. (1989). 'Flexible specialization, work organisation and skills: approaching the 'second industrial divide'. *New Technology, Work and Employment* 4(2) Autumn.

Piehl, E. (1989). 'A review of the developments towards a vocational training policy for the European Community'. *Vocational Training* 1.

Pierce, J. (1967). *Computers in Higher Education. Report to the President from the Science Advisory Committee*, National Science Foundation, Washington DC.

Piore, M.J. and Sabel, C.F. (1984). *The Second Industrial Divide – Possibilities for Prosperity*, New York, Basic Books.

Pollert, A. (1987). '*The Flexible Firm': A Model in Search of Reality or a Policy in Search of a Practice?* Warwick Papers in Industrial Relations 19, Industrial Relations Research Unit, University of Warwick.

Polytechnics and Colleges Funding Council (1990). *Revised Strategic Plans*, PCFC Information Paper, London, PCFC.

Raggatt, P. and Unwin, L. (1991). *Change and Intervention: Vocational Education and Training*, Lewes, Falmer Press.

Raven, J. (1991). 'Management for a purpose'. Conference paper for *The Management of Higher Education*, Manchester Business School, January 1991.

Reid, E. (1990). 'Further and Higher Education'. In R. Morris (ed.) *Central and Local Control of Education After the Education Reform Act*, London, Longmans.

Reynolds, P.A. (1986). 'Foreword' to the report of the CVCP group on academic standards, *Academic Standards in Universities: Universities' Methods and Procedures for Maintaining and Monitoring Academic Standards in the Context of the Quality of their Teaching*, London, CVCP.

Rich, A. (1975). 'Toward a woman-centred university'. In F. Howe (ed.) *Woman and the Power to Change*, New York, McGraw-Hill.

Richardson, M. (1991). 'Governance: the institutional viewpoint'. In T. Schuller (ed.) *The Future of Higher Education*, Milton Keynes, SRHE/Open University Press.

Rivis, V. (1990). 'Educational Guidance for Adults: An overview of principles and practice in the European Community' (Unpublished observations).

Robbins Report (1963). *Higher Education*, Report of the Committee under the Chairmanship of Lord Robbins, Cm 2154, London, HMSO.

Royal Society of Arts (1989). *New Governors for Further Education*, London, RSA.

Royal Society of Arts (1990). *Higher Education for Capability*, London, RSA.

Rumble, G. (1986). *The Planning and Management of Distance Education*, London, Croom Helm.

Russell Report (1973). *Adult Education: A Plan for Development*. A report by a Committee of Inquiry appointed by the Secretary of State for Education and Science under the Chairmanship of Sir Lionell Russell, CBE, London, HMSO.

Schmidt, H. (1990). 'The United Nations'. *The Listener* 123, No. 3164, 10 May.

Schuller, T. (1991). 'Reassessing the future'. In T. Schuller, (ed.) *The Future of Higher Education*, Milton Keynes, SRHE/Open University Press.

Schuller, T., Tight, M. and Weil, S. (1988). 'Continuing education and the redrawing of boundaries'. *Higher Education Quarterly* 42(4).

Scott, P. (1984). *The Crisis of the University*, London, Croom Helm.

Scott, P. (1990). 'Adrift in the rapid currents', Review of the Year 1990, *Times Higher Education Supplement*, 28 December.

Sheffield University Innovations in Learning Group (1990). *The Bulletin of the Innovations in Learning Group*, Spring, Sheffield University.

Shirley, S. (1987). 'The distributed office', *Journal of the Royal Society of Arts*, June.

Slee, P. (1989). 'A consensus framework for higher education'. In C. Ball and H. Eggins (eds) *Higher Education into the 1990s*, Milton Keynes, SRHE/Open University Press.

Slee, P. (1990). 'Apocalypse now? Where will higher education go in the twenty-first century?' In P.W.G. Wright (ed.) *Industry and Higher Education*, Milton Keynes, SRHE/Open University Press.

Squires, G. (1987). 'The Curriculum'. In T. Becher (ed.) *British Higher Education*, London, Allen & Unwin.

Stubbs, W. (1991). 'Governance and sectoral differentiation'. In T. Schuller (ed.) *The Future of Higher Education*, Milton Keynes, SRHE/Open University Press.

Storey, J. and Sisson, K. (1990). 'Limits to transformation: human resource management in the British Sector'. *Industrial Relations Journal* 20(1).

Steedman, H. (1988). 'Vocational training in France and Britain: mechanical and electrical craftsmen'. *National Institute Economic Review* No. 8.

Tansley, P. (1989). *Course Teams: The Way Forward in Further Education?* Slough, NFER.

The Higher (1991). 'Big sixth forms fail the grade', 16 August.

Thomas, K. (1988). 'The past in a clearer light'. *Times Higher Education Supplement* 2 December.

Thorne, D. (1991). 'Learning outcomes and credits in Higher Education', Seminar to Centre for Youth and Adult Studies, Open University, 17 June 1991.

Tight, M. (1988). 'Institutional typologies'. *Higher Education Review* 20(3).

Times Educational Supplement (1990). 'Agreement between Ford and its Trade Unions'. Report on the publication of the Ruskin College Trade Union Research Unit on the Employer Development and Assistance Programme (EDAP), 31 August.

Training Agency (1990). *The Training and Development of Trainers*, Sheffield, T.A.

Trow, M. (1981). 'Comparative perspectives on access'. In O. Fulton (ed.) *Access to Higher Education*, Guildford, SRHE.

Trow, M. (1989). 'The Robbins trap: British attitudes and the limits of expansion'. *Higher Education Quarterly* 43(1).

Unit For The Development of Adult and Continuing Education (1990). *Performance Indicators and the Education of Adults*, Leicester, UDACE.

Unit For The Development of Adult and Continuing Education (1991). *What Can Graduates do?* Leicester, UDACE.

Unwin, L. (1991). 'Reaping the industrial benefits: NVQs and the man-made fibres industry'. In P. Raggatt and L. Unwin (eds) *Change and Intervention: Vocational Education and Training*, Lewes, Falmer Press.

Van Hoof, J.J. and Van Wieringen, A.M.L. (1986). 'Cooperation, Competition and Corporation: the emergence of a new pattern of relations between education, industry and the state in the Netherlands'. In D.L. Parkes *et al.* (eds) *Education, Training and Labour Market Policy*, SVO.

Varlaam, C. (1987). *Contract Researchers in Universities*, Brighton, Institute of Manpower Studies.

Warnock, M. (1989). *Universities: Knowing our Minds*, London, Chatto & Windus.

Watts, A.G., Dartois, C. and Plant, P. (1986). *Educational and Vocational Guidance Services for the 14–25 Age-Group in the European Community*, EEC Directorate General for Employment, Social Affairs and Education (Social Europe Supplement 4/87), Brussels.

Weaver, T. (1979). 'Department of Education and Science: *Central* Control of Education?' Unit 2 E222 *The Control of Education in Britain*, Milton Keynes, The Open University.

Weaver, T. (1983). 'Policy options for post-tertiary education'. In O. Boyd-Barrett *et al.* (eds) *Approaches to Post-School Management*, London, Harper & Row.

Whitehead, A.N. (1932). *The Aims of Education and Other Essays*, London, Williams and Norgate.

Williams, P. (1990). Report of an interview with the *Times Higher Education Supplement*, 6 July.

Wright, P.W.G. (1990). 'Introduction: crossing the border or creating a shared territory?' In P.W.G. Wright (ed.) *Industry and Higher Education*, Milton Keynes, SRHE/Open University Press.

Yates, I.R. (1990). 'Review of recent developments and forward look to the year 2000'. Paper presented to the SRHE Annual Conference.

Index

élite
  academic élite, 62
  attitudes and concepts, 17, 24, 28
  mode of higher education, 5, 28
  tradition, 46
élitism, 63, 120
élitist system, 43
employment, 40, 44
  growth areas of, 97
  preparation for, 54
  prospects of, 98
  relevance to, 54–5
  trends, 119
  world of, 58, 61
England, 5, 50–1, 62, 72–9, 104, 124, 148
enterprise, 10, 17, 76
entrepreneurial
  approach, 11
  income, 7
entrepreneurialism, 120
environmental issues, 55, 56, 64, 83, 88, 161
equal opportunities, 87, 166
equality, 91, 120, 148
  equality of funding, 46
equality of employment, 88
ERA (Education Reform Act 1988)
  and adult education, 149
  and further education, 57, 61, 69, 70, 79, 81
  and higher education, 49, 54, 55
  and LEAs, 70, 105–8
  legislation as change model, 6, 77, 132
  loss of tenure, 30
  and polytechnic corporate status, 40–2, 146, 153–5
Europe, 72–81, 82–93, 161, 166
  impact on funding curriculum, 150, 151
  union, 16, 65, 92
evaluation, 4, 43, 56, 131, 162, 163
examining bodies, 74, 78
excellence, 9, 43, 73, 120, 160
expansion, 28, 43–6, 54, 87–8, 106, 112, 119–25, 124

fees
  and access, 5, 6
  economic, full-cost, 20, 122, 123
  fees-only students, 9
  as a funding device, 147
  part-time, 111
  and sponsors, 162
  top-up, 154
FEFC (Further Education Funding Councils), 105, 148

FEU (Further Education Unit), 63, 98, 131, 132, 149
Finland, 148
flexibility, 61, 68, 120, 155
flexible attitudes, 92
France, 73–9, 83, 114, 138, 148, 164
franchising, 47, 52, 57, 126
freedom, 21, 25, 30, 34, 39
funding
  of adult education, 132–3
  bodies, 19, 149, 155, 162
  changes, 54, 107, 143, 146–7, 153–5
  from Europe, 150
  of polytechnics, 44–6, 106–7, 153–5
  private, 155, 165
  specific, 131, 149
  for staff development, 102
  TECs, 112–14

Germany, 24, 72–9, 109, 163, 164
governing bodies, 76–7, 107–8, 127, 146, 155
grants to students, 7, 15, 110, 119, 147
Greece, 74
growth, 119–26, 150, 154
  and change, 52, 55
  of polytechnics, 40, 41

hierarchy, 18, 55, 56, 96, 97, 153
highly qualified people, 54, 55, 90, 122, 125
HMI (Her Majesty's Inspectorate), 6, 45, 112, 127, 129, 130, 145

income generation, 31
incorporation, 57, 153, 159
innovation, 58, 59, 154
  in curriculum, 79
  in Europe, 85
  in teaching and learning, 46, 58
investment
  capital, 95, 154, 155
  failure of, 17
  government, 15
  as input act of faith, 10, 143
  lack of, 73, 85
  need for, 78, 81, 122
  in training, 44
  in updating (France), 79
IT (Information Technology), 48, 54, 60, 66, 69–70, 85, 88, 140, 148
Italy, 74, 83, 114

Japan, 24, 72, 163
Jarratt Report, 9, 17, 19, 156